D0168650

Advance Praise for
Shower of Heavenly Roses _____

"*Shower of Heavenly Roses* is a rich collection of stories of the friendship of St. Therese of Lisieux. These modern women and men whose lives have been changed by the Little Flower's intercession are articulate and fascinating witnesses to the absolute reality of what Catholics call the Communion of Saints: the life-giving power of God's love, breaking the boundaries of even time and space."

–Amy Welborn, author of *The Words We Pray: Discovering the Richness of Traditional Catholic Prayers*

"This book is the perfect *gift* book. Oh sure, it's great to read for yourself, but all the way through I kept thinking, I've got to send one to Barb, and Euli will like one, and maybe Peter? Mom for sure, and it wouldn't hurt to buy a couple to have on hand for Christmas gifts. Yes, this is definitely a gift book."   –Sister Patricia Proctor, OSC, author of *101 Inspirational Stories of the Rosary*

"St. Therese of Lisieux compared herself to a 'little flower,' and unfortunately this image has, over the decades, become slightly sappy and romanticized. On the contrary, for Therese the 'little flower' image was one of strength and endurance, like the flower that pushes up through a crack in a rock and thrives. This is the St. Therese we meet in Elizabeth Ficocelli's book, in the frequently astonishing, always inspiring stories she collected. This is the Therese who understood well the biblical image of God's 'mighty arm' (Psalm 89:13), and she is with us still and active in the risen Lord. Read these pages and rejoice.

–Mitch Finley, author of *The Joy of Being Catholic*

"Thank you, Elizabeth Ficocelli, for giving us *Shower of Heavenly Roses*. This powerful book will touch the hearts of everyone. It reawakens our hearts to the fact that God's love for us is real. Every page is filled with lines of comfort and stories of peace and hope. Enjoy!"

–Mary Ellen "Angel Scribe,"
author of *Expect Miracles*

"As a lifelong fan of St. Therese, I offer an enthusiastic 'Thumbs Up!' for *Shower of Heavenly Roses*. The stories of her intercessions range from tender to stunning, and involve such ordinary people that any reader will feel right at home. Author Elizabeth Ficocelli has done a wonderful job helping us get to know this thoroughly modern saint."

–Joan Wester Anderson, author of the
New York Times bestseller *Where Angels Walk*
and *In the Arms of Angels*

"Through Elizabeth Ficocelli's *Shower of Heavenly Roses*, readers will marvel at all the Lord continues to do in our lives through St. Therese, 'the greatest saint of modern times.'"

–Fr. Donald Kinney, OCD, Chairman,
St. Therese Relics in the U.S.A Committee

"*Shower of Heavenly Roses* is a beautiful work of love, written in a gentle, quiet style. Each individual story truly witnesses the faithful devotion millions of people have to the Little Flower." –JoLynn Adams, Theresian World Ministry

February 14, 2017

Dear Theresa,

SHOWER OF
HEAVENLY
ROSES

Miracles are all around us — few are extraordinary and most are in the common happenings of day to day life — we just need to look for them and say "thank you Lord."

Enjoy picking up this book from time to time for a little uplift.

Lots of love,
Caroline & Don

SHOWER OF HEAVENLY ROSES

Stories of the Intercession of
St. Therese of Lisieux

ELIZABETH FICOCELLI

A Crossroad Book
The Crossroad Publishing Company
New York

The Crossroad Publishing Company
www.CrossroadPublishing.com

Copyright © 2004 by Elizabeth Ficocelli

All rights reserved. No part of this book may be reproduced, stored in a retrieval system, or transmitted, in any form or by any means, electronic, mechanical, photocopying, recording, or otherwise, without the written permission of The Crossroad Publishing Company.

Printed in the United States of America

Library of Congress Cataloging-in-Publication Data
Shower of heavenly roses : inspirational true stories of healings / [edited by] Elizabeth Ficocelli.
    p. cm.
    Includes bibliographical references.
    ISBN 0-8245-2256-7 (alk. paper)
    1. Miracles – Case studies. 2. Spiritual healing – Case studies. 3. Thérèse, de Lisieux, Saint, 1873–1897. I. Ficocelli, Elizabeth.
    BT97.2.S565 2004
    282′.092 – dc22

                               2004016522

This printing: December 2015

This book is lovingly dedicated to Mildred Bloomrosen, my second grade teacher and the first to nurture the budding writer within me.

"I feel that my mission is about to begin, my mission of making others love God as I love Him, my mission of teaching my little way to souls. If God answers my requests, my heaven will be spent on earth up until the end of the world. Yes, I want to spend my heaven in doing good on earth. . . . After my death, I will let fall a shower of roses."

— St. Therese of Lisieux
(1873–1897)

CONTENTS

ACKNOWLEDGMENTS

With heartfelt gratitude to all those who shared their souls and their stories, whether they were published in this work or not; to St. Therese of Lisieux, my spiritual sister and friend; and to God, from whom all showers of roses ultimately come.

INTRODUCTION

She is known by many titles: St. Therese of Lisieux. Therese of the Child Jesus and the Holy Face. Doctor of the Church. Universal Patroness of the Missions. Secondary Patron of France. The greatest saint of modern times. And, perhaps most endearingly, the Little Flower.

Without question, Therese is well known.

The question rather, is *how*. How is it possible for a simple young French woman, a cloistered Carmelite nun living twenty-four short years, to intimately touch the lives of millions of souls around the world — *a century after her death?*

The answer, in a word, is love. Therese was a master at love. From her earliest years, Therese was nurtured on love, particularly from her adoring father and motherly sisters, since her own mother passed away while she was still a small child. She, in turn, was intensely passionate in her love, particularly for her family, for nature, and especially for its Creator. Therese loved God with an almost unnatural ability, spending much of her youth in deep contemplation of Him.

It was not terribly surprising, therefore, when a nine-year-old Therese first confided to her father her desire to follow her two older sisters into the Carmelite convent at Lisieux. This desire was not a childish whim; it grew stronger as she grew older. Therese's father knew his daughter well, and while the thought of giving away yet another child,

his precious "Little Queen," caused him great suffering, he
knew that her heart was set. It seemed almost a predestined
arrangement.

To enter the cloistered life before age eighteen was most
unconventional, and there were many obstacles in the process. Fortunately for Therese, what she lacked in age she
more than made up in will. Appealing to the Carmelite
Superior, to the Bishop, and eventually to Pope Leo XIII
himself, she was finally granted permission to enter the convent at the unprecedented age of fifteen. At last, Therese
could live her life dedicated fully to loving and serving
her God.

Age wasn't the only thing that set Therese apart from her
religious counterparts. She ascribed to a rather unique theology, radically opposed to the prevalent Jansenistic view of
her time, which focused on the justice of God and the ne-
cessity of suffering. For Therese, who had spent many years
developing an honest, intimate relationship with her Creator, this image did not suit her. Yes, God was just. But
Therese came to understand that more importantly, He was
a *merciful Father.*

It wasn't that Therese was unwilling to suffer for her Lord.
She had a strong devotion to the image of the suffering Holy
Face imprinted on Veronica's cloth, so much so that she
chose it as a part of her religious name. The Saint clearly
understood the suffering of Jesus as the ultimate expression
of love. She was open to suffering and received it abundantly.

Suffering began early for Therese with the loss of her
mother when she was only four. She was further wounded
by the departure of her surrogate mother, her oldest sister, Pauline, when Pauline entered the Carmel. This loss
was so emotionally damaging for Therese that it brought

on a serious childhood illness that almost claimed her life.
Suffering followed the Saint into the convent. Shortly after
her entry, her father was committed to an insane asylum. It
caused Therese tremendous grief. Throughout her cloistered
life, she was plagued by numerous interior trials. Bearing
these challenges with great patience, love, and silence, she
was often misunderstood by others and further alienated.
But Therese met her challenges with true joy and peace,
and even a sense of humor. She looked for every opportunity to sacrifice, no matter how small, and she did it all in
secret and with great love. There were many such opportu-
nities. Whether doing her chores, instructing the novices or
reciting her prayers, each act caused Therese to grow further in love. She loved flowers and would often adorn the
infant Jesus' altar with petals and blooms from the monastery garden. To Therese, the world was God's garden. In that
garden, she saw herself not as the breathtaking rose or the
elegant lily, but as a simple little wild flower, scarcely noticed
yet growing and giving glory to God.

It seemed Therese could never give enough glory to God.
Her love for her Holy Spouse deepened with each passing
year. Through intense prayer and meditation, Therese came
to understand that God desperately desired the love of His
children, but few were willing to give it to Him. She therefore
begged God to pour out His love upon her without reserve.
This intention was not for her own merit, but simply to fulfill
her Beloved's desires.

Not wishing to harbor this abundant love for herself, Therese longed to share her treasure with the world. Her mission,
she decided, was to make God loved. But how? How could
she, hardly more than a child, achieve such a great mission — *behind convent walls, no less?* While Therese loved

her vocation, and tried always to live it faithfully, sometimes even the religious life seemed inadequate to satisfy
her overwhelming desire to love and serve God.

In her heart of hearts, Therese felt the vocation to be
a saint, a priest, an apostle, a doctor, and a martyr. She
wanted it all, not for self-glory, but to bring glory to God
and His love to all people. Frustrated, it was only through
much prayer that Therese realized the foundation for all of
these vocations, for all of her dreams and desires, was *love*.
Love was everything; it was eternal. For Therese, it was her
true vocation.

It was this love that both freed and empowered Therese:
a fierce love between Creator and creation that was unseen
and unknown by others even in her Carmelite community
and to some degree, by her own biological sisters, now three
in number in the convent. This love, turned outward, became a fervent desire to save souls both on earth and in
purgatory.

With each passing year, Therese yearned to be with her
Heavenly Father, her Beloved Spouse, for all eternity. The
path to heaven was revealed to her one day as she was poring
over Scripture. The words "whoever is a little one, come to
me" burned in her heart in a new and meaningful way.

Therese realized with great confidence that God, the
perfect Father, loved her as a little child. Therefore, she
committed herself to remaining little, humble, obedient, and
loving. By continuing to make small sacrifices and doing ordinary things with extraordinary love, Therese saw that she
would not need to rely on her own strength and merit to
get to heaven. God would simply reach down, cradle His
little child in His arms, and carry her to heaven with Him.

She called this childlike spirituality her "little way," a way of absolute trust, confidence, and abandonment.

Therese's unquenchable devotion led her to eventually compose a beautiful consecration in which she formally offered herself as a holocaust to God's merciful love. Not long after this consecration, she began to cough up blood — the first outward indication that she had contracted tuberculosis and was dying. In the final eighteen months of her life, Therese struggled greatly, inwardly tempted by despair and disappointment that she had failed in her mission. In her terrifying "dark night" she even questioned the existence of God Himself. Though joy was taken from her, her love persisted, her outward countenance was peaceful, and, in the end, she remained faithful.

Therese's body was buried in a simple ceremony, with less than thirty people following her casket to the cemetery. But the greatness of this saint did not remain buried for long. During her last years of life, Therese had been ordered by her Superiors to write about her childhood memories and relationship with God, which Therese did out of obedience. Her three separate manuscripts would later be compiled into one treasure entitled *Story of a Soul*. These writings, capturing the love, suffering, and unique spiritual insight of Therese, were at first shared among Carmelite convents. Before long, however, the writings, like the unstoppable spirit of Therese, flourished outside convent walls in the hands and hearts of the public.

In 1925, within twenty-eight years of her death, public demand was so great that Therese was canonized by Pope Pius XI, who described her rise to sainthood as a "storm of glory." The young woman, he declared, had earned her sainthood not for her great deeds, but for her great love. Her

"little way" yielded tremendous inspiration to millions, earn-
ing her the additional title Doctor of the Church, conferred
by Pope John Paul II in 1997 on the centenary of her death.

It was always a personal dream for Therese to be able to
preach the Gospel on all five continents, "even to the most
remote isles, until the consummation of the ages." She had
a great love for the missions, praying for missionaries and
writing to them often. Although she never set foot outside
of her convent, she was fittingly declared Universal Patroness
of the Missions.

A century after her death, Therese has more than fulfilled
her desire to travel the world and spread God's love to His
people. She has accomplished this mission on three levels,
as simple, unique, and profound as Therese herself.

First, her *Story of a Soul* has been translated into sixty
languages and dialects and continues to inspire millions of
readers of all ages, faiths, and walks of life. Readers find her
message of simplicity and love timelessly attractive. Today,
Therese remains a powerful messenger of God's love to a
hurting world and a model not only for Christians, but for
people of all faiths.

Second, Therese is visiting the world in a physical manner.
To commemorate the hundredth anniversary of her death,
some of the Saint's bones, *holy relics,* have been carefully
contained in an ornate wood and gilt reliquary and have
embarked on a global pilgrimage. The tour began in Lisieux
in 1997 and, at this writing, continues to travel from country
to country as millions of people turn out to demonstrate their
love for this highly revered saint.

When the relics toured the United States from October
1999 to January 2000, 1.1 million people packed into monasteries, churches, and cathedrals from Maryland to Honolulu,

surprising both media and tour organizers. People waited in long lines for hours, eager to get a glimpse of the reliquary or, better yet, to press their hands, lips, or religious items on the Plexiglas surrounding it. Some came simply out of curiosity. Some came to seek healing. But for most, it was a chance-of-a-lifetime opportunity to pay their respects to a dearly loved friend. Many reported the experience to be highly emotional and life changing; a powerful, indescribable spiritual experience. There have been reports of an increase in inquiries about religious vocations, miraculous healings, meaningful confessions, and a return to the faith. Wherever the reliquary travels, it seems to leave in its wake evidence of renewed faith and love and, always, profound peace.

Yet there is third way that Therese has managed to surpass the confines of her convent walls and earthly body to rescue her beloved souls. It is through a promise she made, as she lay on her deathbed gazing at the rose bushes in the courtyard garden. Therese vowed that her work on earth would not end with her passing; rather it would begin. She declared: "I feel that my mission is about to begin; my mission of making others love God as I love Him, my mission of teaching my little way to souls. If God answers my requests my heaven will be spent on earth up until the end of the world. Yes, I want to spend my heaven in doing good on earth. . . . After my death, I will let fall a shower of roses."

This is a promise Therese has kept. For over a century, she has drawn souls closer to God with her message of love and hope. People continue to emulate her simple and accessible way to sainthood as they try to find holiness in their own ordinary lives. But it's more than just words on paper. From her heavenly station, Therese has proven to be a powerful intercessor to those who call upon her. Beginning almost immediately after her death, she has been known to shower the faithful with graces, favors, cures, and other miracles, often leaving her signature calling card of a rose or other flower as an outward sign of her continued devotion. This supernatural phenomenon is the focus of this book. What follows is a collection of stories, intimate testimonials including my own, which illustrate the impact of this tremendous lover of God and of souls. My hope is that the stories will touch you, delight you, inspire you, and surprise you, but most of all deepen your friendship with Therese and especially the God she loved more than life itself.

PROLOGUE

The experience of working on this project has been an unspeakable blessing for me. The outpouring of faith, sorrow, struggle, and jubilation demonstrated in the generous response to my call for stories has been both touching and humbling. There were many moments during the process of collecting, editing, and organizing testimonials into a presentation befitting of St. Therese that I felt entirely unworthy of the task. After all, I am not a Carmelite. I am not a theologian. I am not even a "cradle" Catholic.

Since my entry into the Church over two decades ago, however, I have become deeply involved in and enamored of my adopted faith. In that time, I have immersed myself in the teachings, traditions, and treasures of the Catholic Church. At first, I was irresistibly drawn to intriguing phenomena such as Eucharistic miracles, mystics, stigmata, and apparitions. These were concepts quite foreign to my Lutheran upbringing. Gradually, I felt compelled to study Church history, the sacraments, councils and doctrines, Catholic apologetics (the explanation and defense of the faith), and, of course, the saints.

It was during my introduction to the lives of the saints that I discovered their vital importance to us, not only by the example of their earthly lives, but by their ability to stand before the throne of God and implore His help on our behalf. It was also during this time that I first came to

know St. Therese of Lisieux and recognize the effect she was
having on my life.

St. Therese first put herself in my path, quite literally,
when I was about eight years old. On my walk to school
one day, my eye caught sight of something small and silver,
glittering on the sidewalk. Upon closer inspection, I saw that
it was a religious medal. On the front of the medal was
the image of a beautiful woman wearing a veil and holding
something I couldn't quite make out in her arms. On the
back was a most mysterious inscription, "After my death, I
shall let fall a shower of roses."

As a Protestant schoolgirl, I naturally assumed the image
was that of the Virgin Mary, although I had no idea what the
reference to roses meant. When I showed it to my mother
later that day, she told me the medal probably wasn't very
valuable, but I could keep it if I'd like. This in itself was a
bit miraculous since my parents held a rather poor opinion
of the Catholic faith at the time.

As fate would have it, I tucked the little medal inside
my jewelry box and did not give it much thought after
that. It wasn't until I converted to Catholicism as an adult
and was reading up on the saints that I correctly identified
St. Therese's image on the medal. I suddenly had a gnawing
suspicion that this Carmelite nun had somehow, for some
reason, been keeping an eye on me since I was a child. I
wondered if my finding the medal was part of some plan yet
to be revealed.

This thought inspired me to read St. Therese's autobiography, *Story of a Soul*, and it touched me in a profound
way. I admired the faith and determination of this young
Catholic who overcame her timid nature to sneak into the
restricted areas of the Coliseum in Rome to venerate the

ground where the holy martyrs died or, even more remarkable, who did the forbidden by begging at the feet of a pope
to let her enter the Carmel.

In a way, Therese reminded me of the character Jo from
Little Women. Therese was everything I wanted to be: confident, devoted, passionate, and, most of all, forgiving of
herself. Her life was an adventure and her journey, tri-
umphant. She was a wonderful role model with her "little
way" of spirituality and her intimacy with God, and she
helped me see many areas in my life where I needed to make
changes. I did not, however, call upon her as an intercessor
during this time, because that whole concept was still a bit
awkward to me as a "new" Catholic. The idea of requesting
a sign of roses seemed to me particularly superstitious.

One day, however, while on retreat, I was plagued with a
burning question: Was my mother, deceased for ten years, in
heaven? On the last day of my retreat, I talked to St. Therese in prayer about this question and weakly asked for the
affirmation of a red rose. Almost immediately, a little red
bird landed in the tree outside of my window and began
to sing. I watched intently, wondering if perhaps this was
my sign. A moment later, a young seminarian strolled by
donned in a bright red sweater. My eyes followed him, a bit
more skeptically. Even the sun, I noticed, seemed to have
a reddish glow about it. Now I was convinced I was seeing
things, trying to force an answer, so I left my room to attend
the closing Mass.

After a beautiful worship service, I joined the other re-
treatants in the dining hall for our final meal together. On
each plate, there was a folded prayer card with the picture of
St. Therese of Lisieux on the cover. With trembling hands, I
opened the card, and out dropped a silk red rose. With that,

any doubts I had about the whereabouts of my mother —
or the intercessory power of St. Therese, for that matter —
were erased.

Years later, my oldest son, Michael, came home from
school with an assignment to give an oral report on a saint
of his choice. Naturally, I told him all about St. Therese.
It wasn't until I got to the part about the roses that my
son's interest was suddenly piqued. A rather pragmatic child,
Michael wanted to test the theory for himself.

I asked Michael if he had a prayer intention. "I want to
know if Mrs. Reed is in heaven," he responded immediately.
His answer took me by surprise. I was touched at the concern
Michael still held for the beloved neighbor and surrogate
grandmother he had lost a year earlier. Together, we asked
St. Therese for a sign of flowers to let us know if Mrs. Reed
was in heaven. I told my impatient son he would have to
give some time to let St. Therese do her work.

Two mornings later, when in the hustle and bustle of
busy family life I'd long forgotten our conversation about
St. Therese, the insistent yelling of my son alarmed me.

"Mom? *Mom!*" It was coming from the kitchen. I practi-
cally flew downstairs, recognizing the tone in his voice that
said, *this is really important!*

When I reached the kitchen, out of breath, Michael was
jumping up and down. "Mom!" he exclaimed triumphantly,
"My prayer has been answered! I got my flower! I got my
flower! Mrs. Reed *is* in heaven!"

Bewildered, I followed the direction of his pointed finger. There, on the kitchen table, in a vase, stood a single
yellow rose. My mouth hung open momentarily, and then
I understood. Our weekly Scripture group had gathered at
our home the night before. As usual, Mr. Reed had brought

a flower with him to represent the presence of his wife. He often brought a yellow rose — her favorite — and this particular one was cut from a rose bush we had planted in his wife's honor. In cleaning up after our meeting, I realized that Mr. Reed had accidentally left his flower behind. I was going to run it across the street, but I decided it was too late and I could do it in the morning. I placed the flower on the kitchen table and went to bed, never giving it another thought.

For Michael, none of this was important. The only thing that mattered was this simple yellow rose, specially delivered to him by a heavenly messenger who cared. I shook my head slowly, choking back my emotion. "St. Therese certainly has answered your prayer," I acknowledged. "Not only did she send you a flower, but she sent you one from Mrs. Reed's rose bush! What better sign could you get that Mrs. Reed is in heaven?"

As we hugged, a tear ran down my cheek. But the real miracle for me was not the flower. It was seeing my son so happy and so trusting in divine intervention. I knew this experience would teach him far more than any report for school. His life, like mine, would be greatly enriched by believing confidently in the intercession of saints, one of our great gifts from God.

The Intercession of Saints

About two years after my son's small but poignant miracle of the rose, I was making attempts to segue from a long career as an advertising copywriter to authoring children's books, a dream I've had since childhood. This transition, I discovered, was not as easy as I had imagined. Disheartened by a barrage of rejection slips, I had an inspiration one day to switch gears entirely and write a magazine article about my son's experience with St. Therese. I drafted a manuscript and began submitting it to Catholic publications.

I might also add that it had been a fervent prayer of mine for years that God would use my services in whatever capacity He delighted, for His greater glory. Day after day, I asked Him to use me as His instrument to help bring people to Him. I said this prayer with some trepidation because, in my heart, I hoped He would call on me as a writer, but I truly wanted to be open to *His* plan, not mine.

Then life took one of its unexpected turns. I discovered I was pregnant with a fourth child. We were blessed with three healthy and wonderful boys already. However, I was forty years old now and ready to devote a little time and energy toward some personal writing as my children were becoming somewhat more independent. Another baby, and all the responsibilities that come with that, was not exactly what I had in mind.

As I lay on my living room couch one day, partially morning sick and partially feeling sorry for myself, my husband handed me a piece of mail. To my complete surprise, it was an acceptance letter, only not for one of my children's books. It was an acceptance from *Catholic Parent Magazine* for my story about St. Therese.

It quickly became apparent to me that God was finally taking me up on my offer to serve Him. His time for me was *now*, at age forty, pregnant and busy with three other young children. I sensed that this was the beginning of something special and important, a ministry of sorts. Here was a way for me to do God's work and reach many people, through a creative outlet I loved: *writing!* It seemed perfectly fitting that St. Therese was involved in the start of it all. Soon I had several other Catholic articles published and landed a series of Catholic children's books. God was in the driver's seat, and I was hanging on for the ride. The inspiration for this book came when I received a letter from my aunt. She had read and enjoyed my St. Therese article and sent me an account of her own experience with the Little Flower's intercession. As I read her story and began to hear of others, it occurred to me that a collection of such testimonies of faith would make a wonderful book. With the fervor created by the relics tour in this country and elsewhere, I knew the time for the book was now. I had great peace about the project. *Therese* would handle the details.

I was not able to see the relics myself when they toured this country as I was late with child, but I continue to follow them with great interest. I find the phenomenal response taking place around the world, and especially in our own country, particularly uplifting and significant. We live in a time in which the Catholic Church faces scandal and dissent, shortages of priests and religious, poorly catechized adults, and diminishing numbers attending Mass and receiving sacraments. It seems the world is rapidly becoming secularized. In contrast to this stark reality, a nineteenth-century nun seems to be able to easily draw from people outward piety, devotion, and fervent faith.

Draw me, we shall run after you in the odor of your ointments. This favorite line of St. Therese from the Canticle of Canticles gave her much illumination. She understood that "when a soul allows herself to be captivated by the odor of Your ointments, she cannot run alone; all the souls whom she loves follow in her train; this is done without constraint, without effort, it is a natural consequence of her attraction for You" (*Story of a Soul*). As we lovingly and willingly follow in the "train" of St. Therese of Lisieux and her marvelous spirituality, we must use caution, lest we get (if you'll excuse the pun) off track.

To start, we must understand that saints are gifts from God freely given. They are human beings singled out over history for their exemplary love and obedience who are now in heaven and available for our benefit. It is up to us as individuals whether or not we take advantage of this heavenly reserve. It is not mandatory practice, nor does it necessarily make us better Christians. It is also important to remember that saints function simply as pathways to God. They are never the source of miracles — that's God's jurisdiction.

When we discover a saint with whom we can relate, someone who touches our heart in a special way, our devotion should ultimately bring us closer to God. If it doesn't, something is amiss. We must also keep our heavenly friend in proper perspective. In other words, we may love Therese, converse in prayer with her, honor her as a saint, but not worship her. Worship is reserved for God alone.

In life, Therese never sought her own glory; every gesture and intention was intended for the glory of God alone. She boldly declared she would take her roses before God in heaven for His blessing before she would shower them upon the earth. Everything is subject to His discretion. Therefore, when we call upon the Little Flower, we must not do so in a vacuum. Ultimately, it is by trusting our matters to God, in the example of St. Therese, that our prayers are heard and answered.

Among the personal testimonies in this book, ranging from the ordinary to the extraordinary, you will often hear the term "novena." A novena is a nine-day prayer, a Christian tradition that most likely began with the nine days between the Ascension and Pentecost, in which Mary and the Apostles prayed together in anticipation of the coming of the Holy Spirit. The popular practice of praying novenas to St. Therese is actually not a Carmelite tradition. It was started by a Jesuit, Father Putigan, in the 1920s when Therese was being considered for canonization. As people discovered and fell in love with the personality and spirituality of the Little Flower, this practice was embraced as well, and still remains popular today.

The power of this type of prayer does not lie in the actual words or the number of days it is recited (there is a popular "novena" to St. Therese, for example, that takes five days.) The real strength of a novena is the persistence of faith it demonstrates. After all, it requires discipline and effort to pray faithfully for a period of time.

Jesus Himself admonishes us in Scripture to be persistent in our prayer. However, a formal novena is not mandatory when seeking divine intercession. What *is* required is prayer from the heart, trust, and confidence. Our own words are perfectly adequate. Therese was the first to readily acknowledge her preference for spontaneous and continuous conversation with Jesus over formalized prayers like the Rosary. The bottom line is that prayer is conversation with God, and we should talk in a language that feels comfortable to us and conveys our sentiments.

The practice of requesting a rose or other flower as a sign from St. Therese that a prayer has been heard was also started by Father Putigan. As for the scent of roses sometimes associated with prayers to the Saint, this can be traced back to her original gravesite. Therese was buried in a public

cemetery instead of on the monastery grounds due to anti-
religious laws that were popular at the time of her death.
This turned out to be providential, since her public grave
gave free access to hundreds of thousands of pilgrims for
twenty-six years until the Saint's remains were transferred
to the Carmel chapel at the time of her beatification. Thousands of miracles attributed to the Saint were documented
during this time. When her grave was opened, there were
reports of a pungent fragrance of roses noticeable to all those
in attendance.

The Sign of the Rose

Prudence is required when it comes to asking for roses or
other tangible evidence that Therese is working on a given
situation. We need to keep in mind that Therese did not ask
for or rely on any physical signs from God. She never claimed
to have visions or inner locutions, stigmata or bilocation. In
fact, her faith was put to the ultimate test when the joy
she experienced with God was taken from her during her
"terrifying night," her last eighteen months on earth. Without any affirming signs that there was a God or a heaven,
Therese was able to maintain her faith and receive her eternal reward. We stand to learn a great deal from such a
demonstration of faith.

In Scripture, Jesus cautions us about being a people who
are always demanding signs. Despite the incredible actions
He performed in His day, there were still those who refused
to believe. In the end, we do not glorify Jesus for His miracle
working — we honor Him as the Son of God, who died for
our salvation. In the same way, Therese should not be simply
categorized as a divine deliverer of roses but as a holy woman

who, by countless small decisions and sacrifices, earned her
sainthood and a deserved place in heaven.

On the other hand, this is not to say that God will never
give us a sign. God is God and is free to act as He sees
fit to capture our attention. It is also hard to ignore the
fact that a century after St. Therese left for heaven, the
roses continue to shower down. Some of these roses are
rather spectacular and hard for even the most cynical to
deny: blossoms that never die or lose their scent, buds that
bloom in winter, petals that seem to drop from the sky —
certainly, they are a cause for wonder. As for some of the
more "quiet" occurrences, a skeptic might be tempted to
write them off as a matter of coincidence. When it really
comes down to it, however, what is the difference between
a coincidence and a miracle? The answer is faith, which is
what is so exceptionally evident in the stories presented in
this book.

The subject of requesting signs brings to mind a rather
humorous story I heard once from a man named Bob, whom
I met while on retreat. Bob told me he had injured his back
a few years earlier and had been laid off from work. In his
spare time, as he recuperated in his home, he read the autobiography of St. Therese. The legend he had heard about
the sign of flowers piqued his curiosity. He simply had to
know. Bob decided right then and there to ask St. Therese
for the sign of a bird.

"A bird, Bob?" I interrupted, rather puzzled. Bob shrugged
his shoulders sheepishly. He said he wasn't sure exactly *why*
he asked for a bird, but that was his prayer.

As he lay on his couch, Bob studied the wooden beams
that ran along the ceiling of his southwestern home. A moment later, he spied what he thought might be the tail of a

bird hanging from one of the wooden beams. Looking closer, Bob realized it was the tail of a small lizard common to the area. "I didn't say a lizard," he thought to himself. "I asked for a bird."

After a while, Bob decided to forget the whole thing. At that moment, a little bird landed on the patio just beyond the sliding glass door as Bob watched with interest. The little bird hopped a few steps and stopped. It looked down and picked up something small in its beak. Taking a few more tiny hops, the bird dropped the small object outside the slider before flying away. Intrigued, Bob got up to see what it was. He bent down and picked it up. *It was a flower.*

What can we deduce from this story? Perhaps St. Therese is reminding us that we should take our prayer requests seriously. Or maybe it's her way of letting us know that she still has that marvelous sense of humor as reported by her Carmelite sisters!

One final consideration. The stories you are about to read represent spiritual turning points in people's lives — moments of illumination, gentle kisses of heavenly peace, poignant confirmations when we discover we are listened to, cared for, and loved. They are precious and intimate memories for the storytellers, shared in this book to portray just some of the different ways in which intercession may be experienced.

It is not my intention to establish false hopes by asserting that the intercession described in these stories is either typical or guaranteed. Sometimes, as we've all experienced, prayers are not answered, at least not in the ways we would like them to be, or the answer may simply be no. It is good to remember that St. Therese did not devote her life to asking for good things to happen to her, but rather to asking for the grace from God to handle whatever came her way.

Undeniably, some of the most profound spiritual experiences can come from moments of darkness and disappointment, when the endings aren't happy and we are challenged to look deeper into ourselves and the situation to recognize the will of God for us. We need to have faith, like Therese, that God understands our needs before we do and knows what is best for us in the end. Therefore, do not get overly focused on the roses in the following stories, but relish the faith that has been deepened and the growth of the soul within.

In the end, I think we can all agree there are a lot of wonderful saints for us to study and emulate. Throughout the centuries, the Church has diligently raised up an impressive host of individuals on whom we can model our behavior and spirituality. The fact that John Paul II has beatified more saints in his pontificate *than all other popes in history combined* underscores the importance of these heavenly helpers today.

Yet the extraordinary popularity of one of these saints, St. Therese of Lisieux, is hard to deny. Perhaps the personal connection people seem to experience with her comes from the fact that she is a relative contemporary. She is a woman of our own time. Perhaps it is her complete honesty about her own imperfections and the confidence she displayed that God loved her anyway. This, unquestionably, is a healing and hope-filled message all of us need to hear.

Perhaps, more than anything, it is because God has truly granted St. Therese her desire of beginning her mission after her death. Her message is alive, speaking to us now, working in our hearts and changing them, as God worked in hers. Her shower of roses is falling. We should be rising in response.

Chapter 1

ANSWERS

Ask, and it shall be given to you;
seek, and you will find;
knock, and it shall be opened to you.

— Matthew 7:7

Lost Children

St. Therese, or "Santa Therezinha" (meaning "little Therese" as we fondly call her in Brazil), has had a profound impact on my life. My mother held a special devotion for this saint, calling upon her frequently. One of these times was when I was about to be born, shortly after the start of World War II. The labor was difficult, I was breech, and the doctor told my father he could save the mother but probably not the child. My mother implored St. Therezinha for help, promising that if the baby survived, it would be named after her. The baby lived.

I myself, however, did not come to understand the marvelous intercessions of St. Therezinha until I was an adult diagnosed with a rare type of sarcoma. I went to the United States for surgery and follow-up. Shortly after, there appeared to be a recurrence of the cancer. During this time, I happened to meet some people who were involved in a Theresian ministry. They invited me to one of their meetings, and I was impressed by the spirituality of everyone present. They prayed for me and even assured me that the result of my recent biopsy would be negative — and it was. So I returned to Brazil and formed a Theresian Community, a beautiful organization that has grown strong in number and in good works.

St. Therezinha, my favorite saint, never ceases to amaze me. In addition to sparing my life — *twice* — I feel she also had much to do with reconciling me with my two children after many years of separation.

My two young sons, at the ages of four and seven, were taken abruptly from my care and my country by their father.

He took them to Lebanon, where his family lived. I was devastated. I felt my life had come to an end. After much effort, I obtained "search and arrest" papers and went to Lebanon, only to find he had taken the children to Syria, where my papers were not valid. I spent eight months in Lebanon, trying to contact my husband's family and various authorities, but to no avail. Finally, the threat of a civil war sent me home. I felt defeated, that I would never see my children again, but I did not give up.

Eventually I discovered through a friend I had made during my days in exile that the children spent their holidays in England. This prompted me to go there and hire a private detective to find my boys. It was a difficult process since the English system for entrance into the country requires paperwork only for children over the age of sixteen.

A year later, however, the police located my now ex-husband and sons. My joy at seeing my children again quickly turned to chagrin when I realized my ex-husband had filled their heads with lies about me, and they had no desire whatsoever to have anything to do with me. They were now thirteen and fifteen. I decided to enter into a bitter court litigation, which only resulted in the children being declared "wards of the Crown," which meant they could not leave England. I wrote many letters to the boys at school and visited a year later only to be met with complete rejection. I finally was forced to accept the bitter reality of the situation.

It was only many years later, during my illness and the intercession of St. Therezinha, that it occurred to me to bring my heartache to my new-found spiritual friend.

A few years later, I lost my only brother. By one of those "marvelous coincidences," one of his many friends in

St. Therese helps to find my lost children

Canada, where he had traveled extensively, heard the sad news. The friend contacted another friend in Spain, and one beautiful day I received a condolence note from my oldest son, now thirty-six and living in Spain. There were healing words in his message, and I raced to Spain to be received with kisses, hugs, and lots of love.

Inquiring about my younger son, I learned that he lived in Dublin, Ireland, and we phoned and talked for hours daily. On my last day in Spain, I asked my son if he had any pictures of the two brothers and their families together that he could give me. He had only one, and it had been taken in a pub in Dublin. I almost fainted when I saw the picture.

Hanging on the wall, behind my children and their families, was a picture of St. Therezinha, smiling at me. It was as if the camera had been aimed purposely to include her, but of course they had no idea of who she was or, more importantly, of my devotion and fervent prayers for her intercession. I insisted upon knowing the name of the pub, and I contacted them later. I just had to have their confirmation in writing, although in my heart I already knew the answer. I received an e-mail response to my inquiry if, in fact, the picture on the wall was St. Therese of Lisieux. "Yes," came the e-mail response. "But it is not for sale."

— Gilda Therezinha, Brazil

A Rose in the Snow

I first learned about St. Therese of Lisieux when I was a fourteen-year-old student at a convent boarding school in Westchester, New York. My favorite teacher and mentor, Sister Luke, told me that St. Therese answers our prayers with the sign of a rose. Under Sister Luke's tutelage, I embraced my lapsed Catholic faith with new fervor and was confirmed in the school chapel, taking the name Therese as my Confirmation name.

One snowy winter afternoon, I trailed behind Sister Luke as she walked with a senior student on the school grounds. They were in deep conversation. My eye suddenly spied a single red rose lying on the snow. I remember how very odd it was to see it there. Handing it to Sister Luke, I watched as she and the student blessed themselves, their faces glowing. Later, Sister Luke explained to me that she and the student were discussing the student's calling to enter the convent after graduation. They had been saying a novena to the Little

Flower, and my rose was the answer they sought. The student entered the order that following summer.

My devotion to St. Therese continued through my years at school, mostly due to Sister Luke's passionate devotion and my recollection of that special spiritual moment in which I had played a part. After college, however, religion took a backseat for a while as I tried to sort out new feelings and experiences. I eventually found myself turning back to my faith more diligently in an effort to better cope with the challenges of adult life. I recalled the incident in the snow and prayed to St. Therese for guidance.

Soon after, my sister's father-in-law died suddenly. I had told my sister, Margie, about the rose incident, and she was impressed. She decided she would ask St. Therese for a sign that her father-in-law was in heaven. On the evening before the wake, before any visitors or flower deliveries, Margie walked into the funeral home for a private farewell. She discovered in his hands, which were folded peacefully across his chest, a single red rose. No one could explain how it got there. Thereafter, Margie was a true believer.

The next member of our family to pass away was our beloved father. Margie and I prayed for our sign of the rose. When days went by without an answer, we were distraught. Then, one day, as I was walking past a neighborhood flower shop, the owner ran out and handed me a rose. When I asked why he did this his reply was, "because I wanted to." Margie and I slept peacefully that night, knowing Dad was in heaven.

Sadly, a time arrived when I had to ask for a sign for my sister. Margie died of cancer at the age of forty-five. I prayed to St. Therese the night of her death, this time requesting three roses to tell me that Margie was in heaven with our parents. I entered the funeral home early on the first day of her viewing. There were many lovely flowers all around the room where she lay. On a windowsill was a vase containing three yellow roses. Unlike all the other flowers, these had no card.

A later request to the Saint was for a dear friend, Jane, who also died too soon from cancer. Jane was Jewish and had been intrigued by my "rose stories," as she called them, and would often ask me to repeat them to her. When Jane died, I decided this time to ask her directly for the sign of the rose. The evening of her passing, I prayed, "Come on, Jane, send me that rose so I'll know you are in heaven. You know how important this is to me." That evening, while dining at a local restaurant with my husband, I spotted a single rose at the far end of the bar. I asked the restaurant owner, who was a friend of ours, how the rose came to be on the bar and she had no idea. I knew that still another prayer to St. Therese had been answered, this time through my friend Jane.

The greatest loss came with the passing of my dear husband. With heavy heart I waited for my sign, but three months passed without receiving that special rose. Then, one evening, on what would have been our twenty-third wedding anniversary, a close friend took me out to dinner. At the restaurant, the owner seated us and, reaching for a rose from a nearby table, he proceeded to peel off the petals one by one, placing them decoratively on my empty plate. It was such an unusual thing to do, but I was too filled with emotion to be able to ask why he did it. Later I realized that only my wonderful husband could have arranged for such a special presentation. He must have spoken with the Little Flower about giving me the most memorable sign of the rose of all.   —*Lucille, New York*

A Scent of Roses

In December of 1999, the relics of St. Therese of Lisieux visited Dallas, Texas. At the time, I did not really know much about this saint at all. However, my daughter Tracy called me that month to tell me that she and her boyfriend's mother were going to visit the relics. She wanted to know: would I like to come?

Although I did not have a devotion to the Little Flower, I certainly had a good cause for which to seek spiritual help. My oldest daughter, Natalie, had suffered the loss of two premature babies. The first, a little boy named Austin William, was born at just twenty-two weeks. The second, a little girl named Taylor Nicole, arrived in the world at twenty-four weeks. Both babies were too young to survive. In my grief, I told myself that God must have needed some little angels in heaven. My heart broke for Natalie, who wanted so badly to have a baby.

When Tracy invited me to go to see the relics, I told her I would accompany her. My thought was to seek St. Therese's intercession. Tracy was planning to go late at night to avoid the anticipated crowds. When 11:00 p.m. arrived, I was already in bed and too tired to go. I called my daughter and told her to go without me, but to be sure to ask St. Therese to help Natalie get the baby she so desperately desired.

With that, I drifted off to sleep. At about two in the morning, I woke up to a strange and very pungent smell. I realized it was the scent of roses. I couldn't imagine where the smell was coming from, as there were no flowers in my room, or in my house for that matter. I was intrigued, but managed to go back to sleep.

In the morning, when I woke, I recalled the mysterious scent during the night and wondered if perhaps I had been dreaming. I was still thinking about it when my daughter Tracy came over to me to tell me what an amazing experience it was to visit the relics. She told me that despite the late hour, the place was packed. She had to wait in a very long line. When she finally got up to the reliquary, it was about two in the morning. Tracy was bubbling over with enthusiasm, telling me all about the Little Flower, about the promise of roses, and about how some people claim to actually smell roses as a sign that St. Therese has heard their prayers!

At this news, I was completely dumbfounded. I proceeded to tell my daughter how I had awakened at 2:00 a.m. to the distinct smell of roses. We looked at each other in amazement. We both felt something really important must have happened. That day, I decided I had to go to thank St. Therese in person for hearing our prayer. I called a friend, and we went to see her relics that evening. It was an awesome experience, so beautiful and so moving. From that day on, all my worries about Natalie were gone. I was completely at peace and knew with great confidence that my daughter would one day have her cherished baby.

In April 2001, Natalie delivered a healthy seven-pound baby boy named Travis. He is my constant reminder of St. Therese's miracle, and I thank this beloved saint and the Lord for responding to my prayers.

Ever since that experience, I call on St. Therese to find she never lets me down. Ten days after my grandson was born, my husband was diagnosed with lung and lymphatic cancer. The doctors said he only had a 15 percent chance of making it through the year. Once again, I implored St. Therese for her intercession and, as a result, my husband has been cancer free now for two years.

I love the Little Flower so dearly. It's funny, I feel like I have known her for a long time although, in reality, it has not been very long at all. I am very close to her spiritually and always feel her presence by my side. She will always have my utmost devotion.   — *Diana, Texas*

A Place of My Own

My father was battling with the return of cancer in the fall of 1997. For several months, he alternated between being hospitalized and living with family members since he wasn't well enough to stay at his own apartment by himself. During this trying time, I took care of his day-to-day affairs by paying his bills, checking on his apartment, and sending the rent check to his landlord each month.

Sadly, Dad passed away on December 27, 1997, without ever returning to his home. I contacted his landlord to let him know and paid one additional month's rent to allow my sisters and me a few weeks' time to clean out the apartment.

Since I had been living back at home with my mother and stepfather at the time of my father's death, the thought occurred to me of taking over my father's apartment myself. Then I decided that perhaps a smarter idea would be to look for a home to purchase, instead of renting. I hadn't been thinking along those lines before this, nor had I been saving up any money for a down payment on a house.

Nonetheless, one cold January weekend only a few weeks after my father's death, I searched the classifieds and started going to open houses. After a few weeks of house hunting, I walked into a condominium and knew immediately that this was the place for me. It was frigid outside and the trees were bare, but as I stood in the kitchen looking out the window, I saw this image of myself living in this house, with the trees outside in full bloom and a warm, spring breeze blowing in the open window. This image only lasted a minute, but it was so real that I felt sure this place would be mine before long.

However, the reality of purchasing my first home as a single woman hit me later that day. As I crunched the numbers, trying to figure out if I could afford the monthly mortgage and utility payments, fear and doubt started to creep in. Each night I prayed to God for guidance, and also directed prayers to my father's spirit and to St. Therese of Lisieux. Although I no longer considered myself a practicing Catholic, I still felt a connection to the saint I had learned about as a child and whose name I shared (my middle name is Therese). I had been taught that if you prayed to St. Therese, the Little Flower of Jesus, she would send you a rose as a sign of her intercession.

So I prayed for some indication that I would be okay financially if I made the decision to purchase this home. My answers came to me in several dramatic ways not long after.

I worked at a public library at the time, and walked into the back room where new books were prepared to go out to the shelves for loan. My eye immediately went to a tall book on the cart, where the word "Therese" appeared in bold, black letters against the white spine. I picked up the book and found that it was about my favorite saint, Therese of Lisieux. I talked to my co-worker who was busy processing those books, and she told me that the librarians hadn't even purchased that one. It was donated to the library by one of our patrons just that week! I took this to be an answer from the Little Flower in response to my prayers. It was such a beautiful coffee-table book that I ended up buying a copy for myself.

Also, the name of the condo complex I hoped to move into was called "Rosewood" and featured an image of a rose on the entrance sign. I thought perhaps I was grasping here, but it *was* something rose-related.

But my coincidences didn't end there. That same week, I was sitting at my desk in the library when my father's landlord walked into my office. We had spoken on the phone several times during my father's illness, so the landlord knew where I worked, but I didn't really know him personally. He said that mail for my dad had continued to arrive at his old apartment. I thanked him for dropping it off but figured there wouldn't be anything important in it as I had been having my dad's mail forwarded to me.

As I sorted through the mail, however, I received the final answer to my prayers. In among the circulars and junk mail, there was an envelope from a charitable organization, one of those places that sends free personalized return address labels along with a request for a donation. It was from a society honoring St. Therese, and each label featured my father's name and address along with a pink rose in the corner. There were several stickers with St. Therese's picture on them as well. My father wasn't a very religious man and probably didn't send donations to charities like that. To me, however, it was as if my dad and St. Therese had joined together to give me the definitive answer to my prayer.

Shortly after, my sisters and I finished settling my father's affairs. Although he didn't have much to leave us, there was a small insurance policy that provided each of us with a little money. I now had something to use toward a down payment. My mother and stepfather also made me an offer. Since they had contributed financially to both my sisters' weddings and I was still single, they said they would contribute the same amount toward my house purchase if I so desired.

With all these events coming together, I felt more confident to move forward with purchasing the condominium. Things moved quickly, and less than four months after my dad's death, I was a new homeowner! On the day I entered my condo for the first time, I stood on the threshold and said a prayer, inviting and welcoming God into my new home. The very first item I carried into my new place was a statue of St. Therese. She stood there on the counter as I moved my belongings in over the next several weeks and, to this day, she is a fixture in my home where I've lived happily ever since.   — *Caroline, Rhode Island*

Therese, on the Job

I have had a devotion to St. Therese of Lisieux since I was a little child. I am now seventy-nine years old. Through the years, many people who know of my love for this special saint have asked me to pray to St. Therese on behalf of their needs, and many times I have received answers.

As a child, I was always making novenas to St. Therese. One time a friend of my mother's was dying of cancer. I prayed a novena for this woman, asking St. Therese to intercede for her. I prayed that my mother's friend would either be cured or that she would have a peaceful death. I just didn't want her to suffer any longer.

Shortly after the novena, I was traveling on the train, on my way to high school. My schoolbooks were piled on my lap. All of a sudden, I noticed that rose petals had fallen on my books. I looked around, but I could not see or smell roses anywhere. When I came home from school that afternoon, my mother informed me that her friend had died that day.

Another time, I was applying for a job at Standard Oil, in New York. I went to the company for an interview and to fill out an application, but they told me that I was too young for the job. They suggested that perhaps I come back at a later date. I was very disappointed at the news. My father, who had passed away before I graduated from grammar school, had worked for Standard Oil. He would have been so proud if I had worked for the same company.

As I left the interview, my heart was heavy. I didn't know what to do. Finally, I decided to go to St. Patrick's Cathedral to pray about it. Inside the church, I couldn't find a statue of St. Therese. "If anyone could help me," I thought, "she could." Looking around, I spied a side altar featuring a statue of St. Anthony. I approached the altar respectfully and knelt down. In my prayers, I offered up my disappointment about not getting the job, but still asked for intercession. As I was getting up to leave, I noticed a rose lying at my knee. I picked it up, curiously.

That day, when I arrived home, the phone rang. It was Standard Oil. They told me I had the job. I was to report to work Monday!

Thank you, St. Therese. You have truly been a friend for life.
                                                    —Peg, Nevada

Flora

An Italian couple from my parish who had been married a few years decided to try to conceive a child. For years they tried, without success. They tried clinics and drugs and still they did not get pregnant.

One day this couple came to me for counseling and to share their grief and disappointment about not being able to bring life into the world. I had a book on my desk at the time about St. Therese of Lisieux. The couple had not heard of this saint. I told them to read the book and to pray to the Little Flower for help.

The couple followed my advice. One year later, they became parents to a baby girl born on October 1, St. Therese's feast day. Fittingly, the proud parents named their baby Flora, which in Italian means "flower."

— *Father Ken, Pennsylvania*

Miracle in Montauk

The first time I vacationed in Montauk, it beckoned me. I knew that someday I wanted to live there, but, with limited finances, I could not fathom how. Several years later, my husband and I took all of our savings and a few loans to purchase some land. My dream was to build a vacation house in the future. His dream was to someday sell the land for profit.

There is a little church in Montauk that I loved to frequent while on my visits there. It is named after St. Therese, and devotion to her is very deep among the parishioners.

It is interesting to note that because of its location at the easternmost end of Long Island, this little parish is geographically closer to Lisieux than any other church in the United States. The pastor at the time, Father Raymond, told us the following story about the church's patron saint.

During World War I, Father Raymond's uncle, Father Bernard, served as a chaplain and visited the troops on the battlefield. Soldiers would tell him that they knew he was coming to them to hear their confession and bring them Eucharist. They knew this because a sister (a term used then for a nurse) told them that he was coming.

Father informed the men that sisters (nurses) were not permitted on the battlefields, but soldier after soldier repeated the same story. Finally, the chaplain began to ask for a description of this woman. He was told that she wore a black veil and a brown dress. They also added that the sister smelled of roses, despite the stench of the battlefield. As the convent in Lisieux had recently released photos of Therese, Father happened to have one in his pocket. Each time he presented the photo to the men, they would cry out, "That is her, that is her!"

I myself did not have a devotion to St. Therese at the time, although two of my dear friends in New York spent great effort trying to convince me otherwise. Devotion to this saint seemed to me so saccharine. I tried to read her autobiography but to no avail. One day, one of my friends, a Visitation nun, said, "Elaine, some day Therese is going to grab you. You will receive her shower of roses and you will know."

One morning I drove to our property and found myself actually speaking to her. "Therese," I said. "If we are really meant to live in Montauk, would you please send me a rose?" Shortly after my return home, the doorbell rang at ten o'clock at night. It was a florist I knew, delivering a small basket of flowers with a white rose in the center. A young man whom I had taught in the first grade thirty-one years before had sent it to me. He happened to meet a friend of mine in Syracuse and learned that I had cancer. Was it coincidence, or was Therese beginning to shower me with roses?

Next, my mother died unexpectedly. In clearing sixty years of accumulation in the house, I found St. Therese prayer cards, prayer books, and pictures in drawers, purses, and pockets. I was not aware that my mother had a devotion to her. But it helped me feel confident that in selling the house, even after dividing the profit with other family members, there would be enough to build our home in Montauk.

Then, the real estate market crashed!

I began to pray fervently to St. Therese. I also began to receive roses in various forms: real ones, roses on stationery and pictures of the Saint. In the second year of attempting to sell my mother's house, I decided to put Therese's picture in every room. If any prospective buyer recognized her, I would sell the house at the price that person offered. One day a woman returned with her elderly Italian mother, who resembled my own. I overheard their conversation as they came downstairs from the bedrooms. "Maria, this isa gooda house. The saint, she is ina every room." They purchased the house at our asking price.

After deciding on the model home to build, we met with a legal advisor to establish a hearing for a building permit. The court date given to us was October 1, the feast day of St. Therese of Lisieux. Montauk is a village whose environmental laws are very strict. We were refused a permit based on an environmental impact issue. There were a number of further hearings and each was on dates significant to St. Therese.

Three years and ten surveys later, we were still not approved. We received a call from our legal advisor. He told me to sit down. "Do we have the house?" I shouted. "No," he said, glumly. Then he proceeded to tell me of a new ruling that would cost us thousands of dollars to dig for Indian artifacts and bones. I thought he was joking. Apparently, during construction of a driveway about a mile from our land, bones had been uncovered. The new law provided that nothing could be built within a seven-mile radius without an archeological dig.

My husband felt it was all over. I, more than ever, wanted to go on. (I was still receiving roses!) But the expenses were going beyond what we could afford. We decided to meet with officials. It was explained to us that Native Americans from a nearby reservation initiated the ruling following an excavation in which many artifacts were found.

I asked my husband to drive me to the little Church of St. Therese. I promised I would only take a minute. I walked down the aisle to her stained-glass window and told the Saint, "If you *really* want us in Montauk, I want three roses before I leave on Sunday." It was now Friday afternoon.

We went to talk with our real estate agent, who was out at the time. His secretary brought us into his office and sat me down at a table. In front of me was a single rose in a bud vase. My body became flushed with heat. "Oh, my goodness," I thought. "Therese is working on it."

After leaving the office, my husband pulled me across the plaza to see a model of a car that we had just purchased but not as yet picked up. As we came across the front of the car, I saw a single rose on the dashboard.

*Church of
St. Therese
of Lisieux,
Montauk,
New York*

On Sunday morning, after Mass, I visited an elderly woman, Bea, whom I had known for years. I sometimes helped her file medical forms. Although I was sure that I sent her copies of the medical correspondence, she claimed she never received them. I began to search for them in her desk and closet safe, but could not find them. It was getting late and I had to pick up my husband at the motel and return to New York. However, Bea insisted that I have a cup of tea. I returned to her desk again to sip my tea when she exclaimed she knew where the papers were. She instructed me to look in the box across the room where she kept important things. When I lifted the lid, I found no papers. The box contained a single rose.

"That's three!" I thought excitedly to myself, but it did not stop there. As I gasped in amazement at the rose in the box, I looked up to see none other than St. Therese gazing down at me! For there in front of me, hanging on the wall, was a sixteen-by-twenty-inch portrait of my spiritual friend. In all the years that I visited Bea, I never saw the painting because a curtained French door was always opened and concealing it — until today.

I drove back to the motel and told my husband that we had the house. "How do you know?" he demanded, incredulously. "Therese told me!" I exclaimed.

Not long after, the Bureau of Indian Affairs ruled in our favor; we could begin to build without a dig. When Bea died, she left me the portrait. When our home was completed, we had it blessed and dedicated to St. Therese. Her picture is in every room. Each time I enter my vacation home in Montauk, I feel Therese's embrace. After all, we live in her house.

— *Elaine, New York*

Bundles of Joy

I am the founder and director of an organization called Prolife Across America. For the past fifteen years, we have been committed to bringing positive, persuasive messages through billboard, TV, radio, and newspaper advertising to convey alternative options to abortion.

In addition to this ministry, which keeps me quite busy, I care for my very sick mother and a rather large family. I am a Third Order Carmelite since 1987, and to help me face what comes my way, I begin every day with the Morning Offering prayer and a novena to St. Therese in thanksgiving for all the special favors for which she has interceded on my behalf. I tell the Little Flower that I am joining with her in praying for priests and those discerning the call to priesthood, again in thanksgiving for the favors granted to me.

I consider my biggest "favors" being the last five of my children. We are the proud parents now of thirteen children, six of whom came to us by adoption and are of mixed races with special needs. We are not wealthy people and live on only one income. Each time I had the "urge" to add another member to our family, my husband panicked. I would always rely on the Blessed Mother and my friend, St. Therese, to pray for either his heart to change or mine. Thus, I consider the last five of our blessed additions to be answered prayers from Our Lady and, specifically, St. Therese.

And yes, I received either the sign of a rose or a beautiful rose fragrance with each one!   — Mary Ann, Minnesota

Front Row Seat

I have been a member of a Theresian community, Theresians of the Rockies, for forty years. In our community, it is our great desire to emulate the "little way" of spirituality that St. Therese so marvelously modeled for the world. Our goal is to seek out little things we can do on this earth to honor God as she did.

Our community practices a number of rituals to honor our beloved saint and share her blessing with others. Each spring, we celebrate a beautiful May Crowning of the Blessed Mother to honor Our Lady as St. Therese so loved and honored her. On the feast of St. Therese in October, we take baskets of rose petals to the Carmelite Monastery in Littleton, Colorado, where services of the Blessing of the Roses are held. Our blessed rose petals are shared with the sick and the dying. We also give them to our families and friends to put in their cars and their luggage. We basically spread St. Therese roses everywhere we can.

Since September 11, our community has taken up the practice of tracing a little cross on every building we enter and each airplane we board to protect it and the people inside from the danger of terrorists. We also bless with a little cross the seat we are in, that the person following us will receive our blessing.

In my many years as a Theresian, I have met a multitude of people who have shared precious stories of St. Therese and how she has interceded for them. Our community as a whole experienced one of these miracles a few years ago, which was a particular blessing to us.

It was 1997, and we were very excited to commemorate the hundredth anniversary of St. Therese's death. In January that year, we made plans for a day of celebration in August at Christ the King Church in Denver, Colorado. At the same time, we began organizing a pilgrimage to the Basilica of St. Therese in Lisieux, France. We planned the details of our trip and set the date for October 19, looking forward with great enthusiasm to visiting the homeland of our patron saint and attending Mass together at the basilica.

As if going on this trip were not fabulous enough, we received tremendous news in August that year. Pope John Paul II announced to the world that St. Therese of Lisieux would be declared Doctor of the Church — on October 19! Never in our wildest dreams did we imagine that we would be present on the very Sunday that the Pope and all of Rome (and much of the world, for that matter) would celebrate such an important day in Church history.

There were thirty-seven Theresians from all over the United States who had the great privilege to be at the basilica in Lisieux that day, along with some three thousand other adoring fans. We were crammed in the very back of the church, together with a large crowd, but we were thrilled just to be there in person.

The next thing I knew, our International Director, Sister Rose Ann of the Order of St. Benedict, suddenly disappeared into the crowd. Minutes later, she returned to take all thirty-seven of us to the *very front* of the basilica, where we sat in a row of seats immediately adjacent to the altar. We were dumbfounded! Sister Rose Ann had spied the vacant seats and asked the choir director if her group of thirty-seven American Theresians could have them. This seemed quite impossible, as we had been told there was no more seating available. In fact, there were thousands of people outside who could not even get into the basilica and were listening to the Mass through large loudspeakers.

All of us Theresians were crying with unbelievable joy as the ceremony in Rome was broadcast over the altar loudspeaker. We could not believe this was happening — and we were in the center of it all! We humbly accepted this wonderful gift, these seats of honor, as perhaps a little thank you from St. Therese herself for all our years of Theresian service.

God Bless you, St. Therese!   — *Agnes, Colorado*

The Statuette

My husband and I had been visiting our doctor for a number of months to get at the root of my husband's physical distress. Finally, after a number of medical tests, we were told that two masses were discovered in my husband's stomach. A final test had to be done to determine exactly what these masses were. Although neither of us dared to say it aloud, both of us worried silently and seriously about the possibility of cancer.

I must share that my husband was born on the feast of St. Therese of Lisieux. The morning of his test, we received in the mail a little statuette of St. Therese, so tiny I could enclose it in the palm of my hand. During my husband's procedure, I held the statuette in my clenched fist, fervently asking her prayers for a good outcome. With the good Lord's help, St. Therese did not disappoint me. The doctor related to us afterward that the masses turned out to be three ulcers in my husband's stomach that could be treated successfully.

I have since related this story to many people of different faiths in the hope that devotion to this special and humble saint will encourage others who need her help. We are eternally grateful to our little Therese for sending us one of her "roses."   — *Anne, Ohio*

When a Child Believes

In 1995, I had a very powerful conversion experience with God, and it changed my whole life. Consequently, I sought to pray more and move closer to Him in many ways, especially through the intercession of the saints.

One day I walked into our parish church rectory looking for prayer cards, holy pictures, and other items. A woman there directed me to the St. Therese novena on a prayer card that was in a basket of "giveaways." I had heard of St. Therese before, but I was not very familiar with her or her miracles. The woman told me about the popular tradition that when a person prays the novena, St. Therese will bless that person with a flower, particularly roses. I love roses anyway, so the idea caught my interest, and I took one of the prayer cards. I am sure I had prayed novenas as a child, but I don't remember praying any for a long time.

That night, I took the card out and I started praying the novena. The instructions said to recite the prayer for nine days. I can't remember what I prayed the novena for, or how I wanted St. Therese to intercede for me. I do remember, however, wanting to believe that God works powerfully through the intercession of the saints. I also remember wanting to receive a flower, especially a rose.

My son was fifteen years old during this time. It seemed, whenever I was praying, he would come up to talk to me and ask me why I was praying. Sometimes, he would just come and sit by me. My son was very interested in the change he saw taking place in my prayer life and my spirituality. We had always been very close, but he was going through those "teen years," and I felt a growing need to stop and chat with him on these occasions, even when I was in prayer.

My son asked me about this particular prayer card, and I told him all about St. Therese and the roses. He didn't sound convinced, and said something like, "Well, if you say so," the way kids sometimes do. I know he thought it was far-fetched or, at the very least, somewhat silly.

That same day, our family was traveling, and we were staying in a hotel in a large city. Our son was into roller-blading at the time and asked me if he could go out to skate since he was bored in the hotel room. It was already late and I hesitated, but I went ahead and gave him my permission. I told him to make sure he stayed on the same floor as our room. He promised and departed.

I finished my prayers, including the novena prayer, and felt a little disappointed because I remembered the woman at the rectory telling me that the flower usually comes sometime during the novena. It was getting later, and I was ready for bed. I began to wonder where our son could be. At that moment, he opened the door, rolled into the room, and said, "Look, Mom, what I found almost right outside the door." I looked at his hand, not at all expecting what he handed me: a little pink silk rose. I was so touched that I got emotional, and he asked me what was going on. I reminded him about the novena prayer and that tonight was the last night.

My son was quiet for a long moment and said, "Wow, isn't that something." I could see that he believed, and I believed, too. I think that little rose was meant for the both of us. We both needed it, because fifteen-year-old boys, as well as moms, need to make those little connections with God.

I still have that little rose, because it was a gift from my son, and a gift from St. Therese and God. Since that special experience, I have prayed the novena many times, and I have received as many roses. Sometimes they are fresh roses. Sometimes they are silk. Each one, however, is special, because I know my prayers are being heard.

—Dora, Texas

Chapter 2

WONDERS

I will give thanks to the Lord with all my heart;
I will declare all Your wonders.

— Psalm 9:2

An Unexpected Wedding Guest

Miracles happen every day, in every corner of the world. This is the story of one of those miracles that touched our own lives on a most special day — our wedding, December 27, 1996.

As the big day approached, my fiancé and I were growing more and more excited about our impending wedding. Final preparations were being made on every front, with catering, music, tuxedos, dresses, and other details keeping our minds and bodies busy. Still, we felt very strongly that the foundation of a solid marriage was more important than the little details of a singular albeit important day in our married lives.

This prompted me to pray a simple novena to St. Therese of the Child Jesus. I had come across this novena when a high school classmate's father was sick with something that doctors from Great Bend to the Mayo Clinic could neither identify nor treat. The preface in the prayer pamphlet stated that the novena was guaranteed to work. Believing that prayer is never in vain (and encouraged by the fact that the prayer was very simple, quick, and easy to remember), I decided I would try the nine-day novena for my friend's cause.

The novena is simply completed by praying the Glory Be, followed by the phrase, "St. Therese of the Child Jesus, pray for us," twenty-four consecutive times. The twenty-four repetitions honor the twenty-four years that St. Therese lived. As my birthday was September 24, and as I had worn that number on countless sports uniforms, I thought it would be easy to keep track of the specifics of the novena. To the surprise of the medical community, my friend's father, who had been bedridden for weeks, awoke the morning after I finished the novena with none of the symptoms that had plagued him of late. The following day, he was completely cleared to resume normal activities and, the day after, he returned to work. It is my firm belief that St. Therese worked a miracle on behalf of this man. Although the family has never heard this story, I know they are grateful every day for that healing.

Needless to say, I learned through this experience the power of faith and prayer — and of the intercession of St. Therese. Therefore, I felt compelled to pray the same novena right before our wedding. As I prayed, I invited St. Therese to be with us on our wedding day and throughout our married lives to help us through whatever trials we might face together. Never in my wildest dreams did I imagine the dramatic response we would receive through the grace of God.

After stating our vows, we chose to light a unity candle and then have a special crucifix blessed. My aunt and uncle brought us a crucifix from Medjugorje, Yugoslavia, where the Virgin Mary has been appearing since 1981. The Yugoslavians have a tradition in which the groom carries a crucifix to the altar to be blessed and taken home, where it is a constant reminder of their wedding vows and a centerpiece for the family's prayer life. We chose to combine this tradition and the lighting of the unity candle while the song "On Eagle's Wings" was sung.

After lighting the candle, we took one step down the three steps leading to the altar and then two steps to the right. As the priest was coming in to bless the crucifix, the photographer snapped a photograph that has become something of a wonder. In the picture stands a figure that was not seen by

An unexpected wedding guest at St. Joseph's Church, Flush, Kansas

anyone at the wedding, yet the figure is substantial enough to block out flowers, the altar, and other ornamentation in the church. The young woman stands approximately five feet tall and is dressed in a gown like Carmelite nuns wear on special occasions. She holds in her hands a bouquet of roses that contains a crucifix, which is a trademark of St. Therese of Lisieux. We truly believe St. Therese came to us that night as a sign of her commitment to stand with us as we stand for Christ as a married couple.

The photographer for our wedding belongs to the Mormon Church. As our explanation was not acceptable according to his denominational dogma, the photographer had the negative, photograph, and camera analyzed by several professionals in hopes that some other explanation could be ascertained. To his chagrin, nothing was found to explain this phenomenon.

St. Therese has been known to shower roses down upon certain individuals whose favors she grants. Although my bridal bouquet was to consist of burgundy lilies, the lilies froze during the short trip from Topeka to Manhattan. They were the only flowers in the refrigerated car to do so. The florist tried repeatedly to reach me, but was unable. At the last minute, she substituted burgundy roses for the lilies. These and other incidents reaffirm to us that St. Therese was indeed the mysterious heavenly guest at our wedding.

Despite growing up in a devout Catholic home, I never understood the power of novenas. These two miracles, along with stories we have heard from many other individuals over the last six years, have made our family firm believers in their efficacy. We take no credit for ourselves in the results, but we glory in our God of Wonders and His powerful intercessors, including St. Therese, who are still at work in our world today. — *Amber and Jarvis, Kansas*

Pink Roses

My mother was the most wonderful woman I have ever known. Her death a year ago to breast cancer has left an incredible void in my life and is a very sad memory for me. I truly believe that if it weren't for my mother's great faith — particularly in St. Therese of

Lisieux — my family and I would never have survived the long, twelve-year battle.

My mother's devotion to St. Therese began when she was a young girl. She chose Therese as her Confirmation name. All through her life, Mom had a strong faith and belief in the power of prayer, and Therese was always her favorite saint. It was this strong faith that helped Mom endure two previous cancers, surgery, breast reconstruction, radiation treatment, and chemotherapy. Oddly enough, the most upsetting side effect of her recovery was her hair loss. This was not due to vanity, however. The loss of her hair was a visible sign that she was ill, and the last thing Mom wanted was to burden anyone with her illness. She was the "rock" for everyone around her: family, friends, and even other cancer patients. The doctors were so impressed with Mom's strength, courage, and inspiration that they actually referred other patients to her for counseling.

Dad can remember many times when their plans were put on hold because Mom was counseling a person who had fallen victim to the horrible disease. These people would call on the phone or sometimes even show up at her door unexpected. They were just looking for support and a shoulder to cry on, and Mom never turned any of them away.

I remember one time when a young woman showed up at her front door. The woman had just been diagnosed with breast cancer and was mortified and very emotional. Mom did not know this woman when she arrived, but it was evident by the time she left that they had developed a strong emotional bond. Mom shared with this woman the details of her surgery and reconstruction. She even put her own modesty aside to show the woman her reconstructed breasts.

When a third diagnosis revealed uterine cancer, Mom was really at a low point. How could she keep surviving the hardship this disease was placing on her body? Her biggest concern was still the burden and stress her illness placed on her loved ones. She prayed to the Lord for strength and healing, but this time she also decided to pray a five-day novena to St. Therese, imploring the sign of a rose from the heavenly garden.

On the fifth day there was a knock on the door. It was a flower deliverer, holding a beautiful bouquet of pink roses. My mom loved flowers, and pink roses were her favorite. Immediately, Mom concluded that a family member aware of her prayers had made the gesture. When she read the card, however, she discovered they were from a local merchant whom she knew casually from shopping in his store. He had learned of her illness and sent the flowers with prayers and good wishes. Mom sent her thanks to the merchant, but knew in her heart St. Therese was behind the roses.

At this point in her medical care, Mom had to switch oncologists. She had a great deal of admiration for her new doctor and felt that his expertise helped to give her added years of life. It did not occur to any of us until after Mom's passing that the doctor's name was Rosenshein, a German word for roses. Perhaps another gift from Mom's favorite saint?

In her last few months of life, Dad would buy Mom a dozen pink roses every few days. When her death seemed imminent, our family prayed a novena to St. Therese to be with her, asking again for the sign of a flower. One day I took five of the prettiest roses from my dad's latest bouquet — vibrant long-stemmed pink roses — and arranged them in a vase on the dresser next to Mom's bed where she could see and smell them. Mom died a few hours later.

After her body was taken to the funeral home, I was tidying up and happened to glance at the bedside roses. To my amazement, I noticed that four of them were still as fresh and beautiful as when they had arrived at the house. The fifth, however, had wilted, shriveled up and turned brown. It was completely dead. I showed Dad the roses and he, too, was stunned. Our family of five had just lost a member, just like this bouquet of five roses. Could this be a sign from St. Therese?

At the funeral, our pastor and good friend, Father Kevin, tried to explain the mystery of the roses. He was like a surrogate son to our family and had a great fondness for Mom. His interpretation was that Mom had taken the rose with her to heaven. I found great comfort in that analogy.

At the cemetery, Dad, my brothers, and I sat in front of Mom's coffin, which was decorated with a large spray of pink roses. Even though there wasn't a hint of a breeze that hot summer afternoon, four rose petals dropped, one by one, from the casket. Three petals dropped to the ground forming a semi-circle, while the fourth one fell onto the rail. At first, this seemed a bit eerie to me, but then it occurred to me what this meant. I believe it was Mom's way of saying, "I'm okay, I'm at peace now." I think it was also her way of passing the strength of St. Therese's prayers and miracles on to others.

The memory of Mom, including her love of St. Therese and her gifts of pink roses, is a very tender part of my soul now. The power of prayer remains a strong part of my beliefs. I, too, wish everyone the faith and hope that St. Therese brings to those who merely believe and pray.

— *Kathy, Maryland*

A Safe Landing

The Little Flower has been a tremendous help to me as a Dominican Sister for over seventy years. I first became aware of this special saint through the example of my mother. She had a strong devotion to St. Therese of Lisieux, and sought her intercession many times on behalf of our family. Perhaps the most memorable occasion involved the safe return of my brother, Tom, during World War II.

An air force pilot on a B-17 bomber, Tom saw a lot of action. On one particularly dangerous mission in Germany, Tom encountered many enemy bombers at the same time. As pilot, he gave the order for all ten crew members to bail out. Before Tom could jump himself, however, his plane was shot several times and left incapacitated. The only way for my brother to survive was to evacuate immediately since the plane was carrying firebombs.

To avoid the advancing flames, Tom had to climb out over the top of the aircraft. This was a difficult feat as the plane was beginning to plummet. As a result, my brother slipped and fell, breaking his arm above the elbow. The pain caused him to pass out and fall away from the plane.

All Tom remembers is that the air seemed to receive him, to sort of catch him on the way down. The thought flashed across his mind that someone was praying for him. In his semi-unconscious state, Tom somehow managed to open his parachute. Perhaps it was an automatic reflex due to the endless drills he and his fellow soldiers had practiced.

When Tom hit the ground, he was fully awake and in pain. He had landed in a little orchard where a caretaker was working. Tom, all wound up in a blood-covered parachute,

B-17 pilot Leo Thomas Green,
who saved himself and
ten crew members in 1942

looked up in time to see two German soldiers approaching
him with guns drawn.

To my brother's surprise, the caretaker told the soldiers
that this was *his* prisoner, and that he would "take care of
him." Tom was certain this meant that he would be killed.
The soldiers let the caretaker have the prisoner and, to Tom's
amazement, the caretaker took him to a nearby hospital that
had a special room for prisoners of war. Tom was greatly relieved to have his life spared and delighted to find Americans
with whom he could recover and even play a little cards.

But the good fortune didn't end there. One day during
his recovery, Tom was talking about his home state of Ohio
with another soldier. The German nurse on duty heard the
soldier mention Buckeye Lake, and immediately she joined
the conversation. It turned out the nurse had a sister who
lived there. Even more ironic, it was discovered that the

nurse's mother was married to a cousin of Tom. This unlikely connection between feuding nations earned Tom and his comrades extra care and better food than the typical fare of black bread and potatoes.

Though he recovered quickly, Tom was still held as a prisoner of war. He prayed he would get home safely. But Tom wasn't the only one praying. Since the day he'd left for the war, my mother prayed devoutly for his safety. She pulled out the "big guns" for this one — her spiritual friend, St. Therese of Lisieux. The Little Flower answered the call. I truly believe it was due to her intercession that my brother miraculously saved himself and all ten men that day. First, he had the wherewithal to give the orders to bail out. Second, if he had fallen back into the plane instead of away from it, he would have perished when the plane blew up. Third, the fact that Tom landed in the presence of a sympathetic German caretaker was an unbelievable stroke of luck.

Now the only thing remaining was to get Tom home. A year had passed since he had been taken prisoner. My mother, still praying daily, told St. Therese if Tom returned home safely, she would donate a statue of the great intercessor to her church. Tom was released shortly after, and a statue was presented with gratitude to my mother's parish, where it was displayed in a place of honor.

After the wonderful example of faith and dedication of my mother, I, too, learned to call on St. Therese in times of need. She always seems to come through.

For example, in my younger years as a Dominican, I served as a teacher. As such, I was often faced with problems to solve involving my students. But one time, the source of my annoyance was another teacher. Beside myself, I stopped in the chapel after lunch one day and asked the Little Flower to hear my prayer and bring me peace. I remembered how particular Carmelite sisters often annoyed St. Therese and how she struggled to rise above these feelings.

As I left the chapel, my class was lined up waiting for me at the door. Doing a quick headcount, I noticed one student was missing. At that moment, the missing child came running up to me and handed me a beautiful rose. He said a lady down the street gave it to him to give to me. The lady told him her name was Theresa. My startled expression was noticed by all of my students immediately. One of the children asked, "Don't you want it, Sister?" "Oh, yes," I assured her. "It is an answer to the prayer I just offered in the chapel. Thank you." I just hadn't expected my prayer to be answered so quickly.

Another time I can recall an immediate response was on my way to a Mass the Bishop planned for Jubilarians. I had just prayed to the Little Flower for help in a particular matter and asked for a sign of white roses. No sooner had I arrived at the church than a lady with a big smile came up and promptly pinned a corsage of white roses on me.

Thank you, St. Therese, my Carmelite friend, for all the great help and great love you've showered on this Dominican.   — *Sister Concetta, Ohio*

Rose-Colored Window

I am a Catholic priest who was ordained in 1996. During my first year of seminary, the pre-theology year, I believe the Little Flower sent me a little gift, a sweet consolation to confirm my vocation.

I have a devotion to many of our wonderful saints, but I have always had a special place in my heart for St. Therese. Her "little way" of sanctity is very refreshing and can be emulated by all. Naturally, I called upon the Little Flower for her blessing on my vocation.

I had been at the seminary only a few weeks. In our chapel at St. Charles Borromeo Seminary in Philadelphia, we have beautiful stained-glass windows. At the time, some of the windows were being repaired. The one directly across from where I normally sat had been removed completely and temporarily replaced with clear glass.

Morning prayers at the seminary began at 7:00 a.m. One morning, at exactly that time, the sun was rising. I looked up from my prayers to see a light coming through the window across from me that was the most beautiful color of rose that I have ever seen. It was never that color before or after that day. What day was it? October 1! Thank you, Little Flower.

— *Father Joe, Navy chaplain,*
USS George Washington

The Dream

On June 7, 1997, I was staying at my father's house in Maryland with some friends while my father was in Europe for a few weeks. During this time, my friend Elizabeth introduced me to St. Therese of Lisieux and gave me a copy of her novena. She told me this was a very powerful prayer. I was intrigued by the story of roses, and immediately began meditating on the novena. I even made a photocopy of it and placed it in my wallet.

Fifteen minutes later, another friend who was staying with us came back from breakfast. She carried in her hands a freshly plucked pink rose, which she promptly placed on the kitchen table. I was astonished. I couldn't believe a response could happen so quickly. But this was only the beginning. That night, I had a dream in which a woman appeared to me. She was a nun, with a beautiful countenance and wearing a brown habit. (It is important to understand that I at this point had no preconceived idea of what St. Therese looked like, as there was no image of her on the novena prayer card in my wallet.) The woman in the dream said to me, "When you die, you will be united with Jesus." She then proceeded to place a set of brown Rosary beads around my neck. (I would later discover that brown rosaries were often affiliated with Carmelites.)

I immediately woke up from the dream at 5:30 in the morning. I told my friend, Elizabeth, who was sleeping on the couch at the time. Her feeling was that the woman in the dream was most likely St. Therese. A few days later, we drove home. After arriving at my friend's house, I asked her aunt what St. Therese looked like. The aunt produced a framed picture of St. Therese that she kept in her bedroom. To my amazement, it was the same nun who appeared to me in the dream!

After this profound experience, Elizabeth and I decided to go to St. Charles Seminary in Philadelphia for a conference they were having on St. Therese. Ironically, they were celebrating the hundredth anniversary of the death of the Little Flower. I sat through the lectures and listened intently as each professor presented a slightly different interpretation of Therese's writings. I distinctly remember one professor who lectured on the suffering of St. Therese. She said, "Where there is suffering, there is mercy." This, to me, is the essence of the teachings of St. Therese.

After the conference, I purchased her autobiography, *Story of a Soul*. I wanted to find some evidence that she used the word "united" in her writings to confirm my vision, as I was still a bit skeptical. Sure enough, I found the words "united with Jesus" throughout her writings. There was more than enough evidence that reflected the same language this saint used to me in my dream. Without a doubt, Therese was passionate about being united to Jesus.

After my spiritual experiences with St. Therese, I decided I wasn't living up to my fullest potential. I always wanted to have a music degree, but had never pursued one. The same weekend that St. Therese was proclaimed Doctor of the Church — October 17, 1997 — I enrolled in college. I now have a music degree (cum laude) and recently have been matriculated into graduate school.

St. Therese has had a profound influence on my spiritual life. I hope that this testimonial will change your life in some way and unite you more closely to Jesus through the intercession of St. Therese of Lisieux.

— *Lynne, Pennsylvania*

I Am

My story is most unusual and it has to do with the St. Therese relics tour. I even wrote to the National Shrine of St. Therese afterward to see if anything similar had ever happened before — but no one reported anything like this. . . .

Several years ago, the relics of St. Therese of Lisieux came to Erie, Pennsylvania, to St. Peter's Cathedral for veneration. Wherever the relics travel, they always create huge crowds, and Erie was no different. I was very surprised when a friend of mine who had left the Church years before asked me if I wanted to go with her to see the relics. This friend had not only left the Church; she found great joy in making fun of the faithful.

When she asked me to join her, I naturally questioned her motives. She said she basically wanted to go for a good laugh. She did not take any of this saint stuff seriously. I, on the other hand, felt a genuine desire to go. I can't say I had a deep devotion to the Little Flower at the time, but I had said novenas to her in the past. It was really bothering me that my friend was going with the wrong heart. I told her I believed she was tempting fate with such a disrespectful attitude, but she was determined to go.

As we approached the cathedral, we encountered a rather large crowd consisting of both lay people and religious. Many of them we recognized. Several people smiled and struck up a conversation with me, but it was the strangest thing — not one person spoke to my friend. It was as if she were invisible. This started to bother her as we stood in a long line outside, waiting for our chance to see the relics. The closer we got to the entrance of the church, the more this phenomenon happened, and the more agitated my friend became.

As we finally got our turn to approach the reliquary, I noticed that my friend was hesitating. It first started as we walked past two enormous bowls of unconsecrated hosts that were set out in preparation for the Mass to follow veneration of the relics. I had never seen hosts displayed like that before.

As we stood in front of the glass-enclosed relics, I reached my hand out reverently. After a moment, I looked at my friend, perplexed. "Well?" I asked. "This is what you wanted. Why aren't you putting your hand on it?" At that point, we both placed our hands on the case.

What happened next was incredible.

I suddenly heard an unmistakable, strong male voice say, "I AM." At the same instant, I felt as though I were standing in a great light that shone down from above, like the sun through a skylight or something. I jumped back in surprise and looked around, bewildered, at the other people touching the relics. None of them seemed to see or hear any of this, even the Carmelite sisters who were standing right next to us. At the same moment, my friend suddenly became ill. I thought she might feel better if she got some air since we were near an exit.

Outside, I told her what I had seen and heard. She had not experienced it, and just the mention of the relics brought the sick feeling back again. She even tried to go back into the cathedral to see if the feeling would subside, but could get no further than the door. I, on the other hand, had to go back inside to see where the light could have come from. To this day, I don't know — there are no skylights in the cathedral, and there were no spotlights in that location, either.

My friend continued to experience that ill feeling for months whenever she recalled our visit. During that time, she decided to delve into the life of St. Therese, to try to sort things out. She didn't talk to me much about it. Almost exactly one year later, however, I received an e-mail from her. She had discovered the National Shrine of St. Therese in Niagara Falls, Canada, which wasn't far from where we lived, and she wanted to visit it. Although I wasn't sure exactly why, I agreed to make the trip with her and another friend.

The Shrine is located on the grounds of a Carmelite monastery that includes a lovely old church, Our Lady of Peace. We attended Mass, and my friend shocked us by singing and participating with great zeal throughout the service. As we were touring the Shrine, I gazed at several of the images of St. Therese that were hanging on the walls. One in particular caught my eye, because there was a striking resemblance to my friend. Even my other friend noticed it.

The monastery has its own relics of St. Therese, which are housed in a small chapel in a separate building. This chapel was set up with the divided sections that you typically find in monasteries, and the relics were over on a side altar behind a roped-off section reserved for priests and nuns.

My friend walked in and sat in this quiet, dark chapel for a long time, just staring at the relics. My other friend and I watched her with much concern. After about two hours, I asked her if she wanted to get closer, and she did. We received special permission to approach the relics, which we did with some hesitation. None of us knew what to expect from her. We placed our hands on the relic case and my friend — who just a year earlier had been laughing at such silliness and was suddenly made ill — was now filled with a warm healing.

We have since returned there several times, once for the visit of the major relics. Again, we spent hours in the presence of this great saint, and my friend brought roses and prayers of thanks. Truly, it is a miracle. Thank you, St. Therese!

— *Carol, Pennsylvania*

The Statue

The Living Insights Center in St. Louis, Missouri, is devoted to supporting the spiritual journey of each individual in every way possible. Therefore, our Center maintains sanctuaries devoted to each of the world's major religions. When a statue of St. Therese of Lisieux was donated to our Center for our Christian sanctuary, I accepted the offer graciously but without much emotion. Frankly, I had never heard of her, perhaps at least in part because I'm a Hindu and a Tibetan Buddhist. However, the experiences I've had personally or witnessed through others since then have absolutely convinced me that St. Therese is present in our Center, that she is a direct conduit to God, and that many people have received miracles as a result of her intercession here.

People who have visited St. Therese at our Center have reported literally scores of astounding stories. As a result, the statue has received local media attention both in magazines and on television. Our NBC affiliate chose to devote a "sweeps week" lead story to these miracles. Approximately five hundred people came to visit her during the following two weeks, and at least twenty-five of them reported experiencing miracles — including physical healings, spiritual healings, and the receipt of roses.

The statue was donated to our Center approximately two years ago. As I drove the statue here, I felt St. Therese come to me and ask me to invite a particular friend to help carry her in. This was, for a Hindu and Buddhist, rather unexpected. If I had thought about it, I would not have called this friend, because I knew he'd been in a bad traffic accident

just a week earlier. He'd been driving a Department of Trans-
portation truck at ten miles per hour in the fast lane when a
careless driver ran into him going about seventy. The truck
was designed to withstand such accidents, so my friend was
not killed, but his back was injured, and he'd been to a chi-
ropractor four times during the week. Despite this, when I
told him that St. Therese had asked for him, he came right
over. We carried the statue into the Center together, which
was not easy to do. Then he picked up the statue by himself
and placed it on a pedestal. Immediately, he turned to me
and said, "My God, my back's been healed!" He's been fine
ever since.

About an hour later, a woman who had been to our Center
once before came to the front door, weeping. She'd been
driving nearby with no plan to visit us, but felt called by a
powerful new presence. An hour after that, another woman
who had also visited us previously called from her home
more than twelve miles away, saying she could feel that a
new presence had just arrived at the Center and she wanted
to know who it was. This was St. Therese's first day here.

Some months later, a woman whose family is very devoted
to St. Therese came to pray for her daughter, who had been
born with a congenital heart defect and was about to have
her third open heart surgery. The woman later decided to
send St. Therese a dozen roses, which she ordered from California. They were to be delivered by an overnight courier
service on a Saturday.

That Friday, the courier delivered a dozen of the most
beautiful roses I have ever seen. They were quite unusual,
as the petals had stripes. Just five minutes after I placed the
roses before St. Therese, the woman unexpectedly arrived
to pray, and I showed them to her. When she saw them, she

*Miraculous statue
at the Living Insights
Center, St. Louis,
Missouri*

said they weren't the roses she'd ordered, despite the fact
that they had come with a card saying they were in honor of
her daughter. She called the florist and they said the roses
she had ordered were still to be delivered the next day, that
they couldn't explain why she had received these roses, and
that she should consider them a gift. The next day, the roses
she ordered arrived on schedule. The surgery went so well
that the physician afterward said he couldn't explain how
he'd been able to complete it without having to implant a
pacemaker in the child.

More recently, a man called and said his dog had just been diagnosed with terminal cancer. The veterinarian said the dog was so far gone he might not even make it home. The man asked if he could bring the dog to visit St. Therese, and I said he could. The dog visited us twice. Three weeks later, the man called to tell me that two things had happened. First, the dog was now cancer-free. Second, the dog's trainer had heard of the healing. Her family had a painting of St. Therese that her grandfather painted for a church, but it was never delivered because the priest who requested the painting died before it was completed. When the family heard of the dog's recovery, they decided to donate the painting to our Center. I speculate this was part of what St. Therese had in mind when she interceded in the first place. Now, six months later, the dog is still fine.

Many other miracles have been reported here, and I look forward to many more.   —*Jack, Missouri*

My Mother's Miracle

St. Therese is the patron saint of the parish in which I was raised. As our patroness, she has had a tremendous effect on our family.

It all started with my mother, who converted to Catholicism when she married my father in 1962. They became members of St. Therese Parish in Uniontown, Pennsylvania, where my mother developed a strong devotion to the Little Flower. She called on this saint often to guide and watch over her family.

In 1994, my mother was diagnosed with breast cancer. After a mastectomy and intense radiation — and lots of prayers — she was declared cancer-free. Just at the five-year mark when we thought we were out of the woods in terms of the cancer coming out of remission, we received devastating news. A lump was found behind my mother's lung, which was inoperable due to its location. The cancer was spreading rapidly into her adrenal gland. The doctors gave my mother less than six months to live, with much anticipated pain.

We are a close family and have inherited my mother's faith and devotion to St. Therese. Immediately, our prayers went out to the Little Flower for help. We prayed first and foremost for my mother to be cured with a miracle. If that were not possible, however, our prayer was for her to live without pain and be able to enjoy each day she had left.

My mother underwent radiation, which worked well on the tumor on her lung. The cancer, however, started to spread through her spine to the brain. Our prayers continued and intensified. A few months later, she had Gamma Knife surgery on her brain, which was successful, and then underwent additional chemotherapy to deal with the rest of the cancer.

Despite the doctor's dire prediction about pain, my mother miraculously did not seem to suffer any. Rather, she surprised all of us by living past the six-month mark and then on past a year. Things were actually beginning to look better until my mother had a seizure due to a new tumor that had developed on her brain. A second brain operation was performed. At about eighteen months after the terminal cancer had been diagnosed, we all realized — including my mother — that we were losing the battle. I went to visit her on Labor Day, and, together, we made a Thanksgiving meal with all the trimmings because we knew she would not make it to November.

A perfectly preserved rose is a continuing reminder
of my mother – and St. Therese

Early on the evening of September 30, 2001, our priest came to the hospital to give my mother her final anointing. She passed away at 6:10 a.m., at sunrise, on October 1, the feast of St. Therese. The miracle of her passing away on this date has helped our family deal with our grief and pain. We believe that St. Therese was instrumental in blessing my mother with a good quality of life for an extended period of eighteen months. We are also confident that this beloved saint was watching over my mother during her ordeal and is with her now in heaven.

There was another very significant miracle in the story, however. On the day we found out about the devastating news of my mother's terminal cancer, my father brought home a yellow rose for his wife, which he carefully placed in a vase on the dining room table next to my mother's favorite statue of St. Therese. All during my mother's eighteen-month battle with cancer, the rose did not die. Rather, it seems to have preserved itself perfectly, retaining its color and delicate form. Almost three and a half years later, the rose still stands next to that statue. It is a lasting reminder to all of us of my mother's miracle.   — *Paula, Ohio*

Thrift Shop Visitor

My husband, Mike, is a Vietnam veteran and the Commander of the Disabled American Veterans Chapter in Prescott, Arizona. The Chapter runs a local thrift shop, and when the person in charge of it left, Mike stepped in to run it. I was worried about Mike doing this, since he is not a well man and should not have been working at the thrift shop on such a regular basis.

One day Mike was working at the shop. There were two women volunteers working in the back room, sorting through deliveries, pricing items, and making sewing repairs. Mike had his back to the front door while he was dusting some shelves in front of the counter when he suddenly felt a light tap on his shoulder. It startled him, because he had not heard the bell on the front door.

He turned around to find a young woman, who was not very tall, with brown hair, no makeup, jeans, a loose-fitting shirt, and a baseball cap, holding a bag. She said to him, "I would like to donate these things." Mike said, "Okay, let me take them and put them on the counter." The bag was heavy, and he set it on the counter and turned around to thank the woman, but she seemed to have vanished. He called to the women in the back room, asking if they had just seen someone there. The women confirmed they had, but they did not see her leave and did not hear the bell on the door either time.

Bewildered, Mike called me at the nursing home where I live because of my medical infirmities. He said the weirdest thing had just happened and told me about it. I asked him if he had looked in the bag. When he said he hadn't, I told him to open the bag and tell me what was inside.

The bag contained a few items of clothing, some paper-back books, and a sealed box. I told my husband to open the box. Mike wasn't sure about doing this, in case the box was left by mistake, but at my prodding, he opened it. He reported that the box contained a beautiful statue of an angel. It stood fourteen inches tall, with a wingspan of about twelve inches. The statue was hand-carved out of ivory and appeared quite old.

I confided to my husband that I had been praying for him about his declining health and the anguish he was going through. I had prayed a novena to St. Therese of the Child Jesus and also directed my prayers to St. Michael, my husband's namesake, to send Mike help. I explained to my husband that the statue was St. Michael the Archangel. I said, "Sweetheart, the statue is meant for you in answer to my prayers. You need to bring it here to the nursing home, and I will get it blessed so you can take it home."

After he closed the shop that day, Mike reluctantly brought the statue with him to see me. He still was not sure the statue should be his. He handed me the statue, and I inspected the incredible detail, amazed at how each feather on Michael's wing looked almost real.

In my room, I have a number of pictures on my wall of the Blessed Virgin in many of the various ways she is depicted. Among them, I also have a picture of St. Therese of the Child Jesus to whom I had made the novena. As I gazed at the statue in my hands, I said to Mike, "Look at all the pictures on my wall, and tell me if you recognize any of them." At the time, my husband was not Catholic and would not have known the Blessed Virgin from Brigitte Bardot. He walked right over to the far left corner of my room and pointed his finger upward at the picture of St. Therese and said in amazement, "That's her, that's the woman from the thrift shop." He turned to me, asking if that was Mary.

"No," I replied. "That's St. Therese of the Child Jesus to whom I have prayed since I was a child. She and I go way back, and occasionally she does me a favor. I told her about you and how worried I am about your health, so she sent you

St. Michael the Archangel. That's why I know this statue is for you. I'll get him blessed, and you can take him home and find him a place of honor."

My husband did just that. He took the blessed statue home and placed a beautiful plant next to it. He tells me, it's really strange, but there is never any dust on the statue or the plant. Mike converted to Catholicism and was baptized during a Mass that was said for my reception into the Lay Carmelites. This is really a miracle because Mike had always felt that there was no redemption for him because of what he experienced in Vietnam and because of his deteriorating health. Today, Mike prays to St. Michael regularly and, when he dreams of Vietnam, where he served three tours of duty, he invokes the power of St. Michael the Archangel to help him overcome the nightmares.   — *Dawn, Arizona*

Aunt Mayme's Vision

My dad had one sister and one brother. His brother, Raymond, was diagnosed with tuberculosis at the age of twenty-five, and was sent to a TB sanitarium in Beaver Falls, Pennsylvania. I still have a beautiful tiny leather and beaded handbag with drawstrings that my Uncle Raymond made for my mother as one of his activities in the sanitarium. He also made beaded lampshades, which I remember seeing in my parents' home as a child.

Uncle Raymond was allowed, on occasion, to come and visit us in a suburb of Cleveland, Ohio, where we lived at the time. Although his seven nieces and nephews loved him

dearly, we were never allowed to kiss him. My mother kept
his dishes separate and sterilized them after every meal.
My Aunt Mayme told me that for ten years she prayed
daily to St. Therese, who died from tuberculosis, for a healing
for their brother. Since his health continued to fail, she came
to the conclusion that she was praying for the wrong favor
and began to pray instead for a happy death for Uncle Ray.

For five more years, my uncle continued his downward
spiral, and eventually my dad and Aunt Mayme were called
to be with him in his last hours in the sanitarium. His room
was located at the end of a long corridor. Because of the
disease, the rooms were kept quite cool, and periodically my
aunt would go out into the hall and stand with her hands
over the steam radiator. The view out of the window there
was as drab as the situation: all she could see was a flat,
black tarred roof.

One night, however, as she was warming her hands by
the radiator, she saw beyond the windows a beautiful green
meadow, with a bower of roses and three steps. To her surprise and delight, St. Therese stood on the top step, facing
the area of my uncle's room. This vision remained there
all night.

At 6:00 a.m., when my aunt returned to warm her hands,
she noticed that St. Therese was now standing on the bottom
step, with both arms extended toward my uncle's room. At
6:15 a.m., just minutes later, my Uncle Raymond went home
to God at the age of forty. My Aunt Mayme was certain that
St. Therese had come to accompany him on his journey.

I was only a child of fifteen when all of this happened,
and I am now eighty-three, but I remember this story as
vividly as if it took place yesterday. I believe God rewarded
my aunt's deep faith and perseverance by sending the Little

Flower to bring her brother home. I have remained devoted
to St. Therese ever since.   — *Trudy, Massachusetts*

The Trailer

Three years ago, I prayed to St. Therese of Lisieux,
asking her to intercede for me. St. Therese has been a
very special saint to me since my teens, and I wanted
to ask her to help me find a house.

I have longed for a house of my own all my life — something to give me a tangible feeling of security, something I
could leave to my children. On the last day of the novena,
my son and I came across a very interesting trailer. We had
been looking at a lot of trailers over the weeks, and both of
us were getting rather discouraged, for none of them seemed
to feel right.

I had just been approved for disability from Social Security, and the money they gave me was going fast. I was
very concerned that I would have nothing left with which
to purchase a home. However, when my son and I entered
this particular trailer, we both liked it immediately, and my
hopes were raised.

While I went down the hallway to check out the bathroom, I could smell an intense aroma of flowers, although I
had not seen any in the trailer. The closer I got to the bathroom, the stronger the aroma became. When I entered the
bathroom, the feeling of "being home" was overwhelming to
me. I looked with surprise at the walls — they were completely covered with rose wallpaper. Here I was, standing in
the middle of this bathroom, surrounded by paper roses and,

as strange as this may sound, it smelled just like freshly cut roses. I called my son in, and he smelled it, too. We walked out, amazed, and I wanted the trailer more than ever.

The man who owned the trailer wanted cash for it. I was quite a bit short of what he was asking, and I had a sinking feeling that buying this trailer would be impossible. My son and I left, disappointed. I could not forget the wallpaper or the fact that I had just prayed a novena to St. Therese. That trailer was meant to be mine, I felt sure of it, but how could I get it without enough money?

On our way home, we ran into an old friend. In our conversation, we told him about the trailer. He invited us to have some coffee with him. As we relayed the story, with the details about the cost, this friend all of a sudden asked to see the trailer. Both my son and I were eager to go back, so we took him there. This time, when I entered the bathroom, I no longer smelled the roses.

After looking at the trailer, my friend asked me how much money I had to put down on it. I only had $2,000 and the trailer was selling for $7,000. My friend calmly gave the owner of the trailer the needed difference, and the trailer was purchased. Over the last three years, I have paid back the money my generous friend lent me, and now the trailer is 100 percent mine.

I did not ask for the loan; all of this was because of St. Therese. She has always been there for me, in the good times as well as the bad. She has interceded on my behalf many times and, because of her, I now have a home that I can give to my children after I am gone. Knowing that my children will always have a home, a place of security, is a great comfort to me. So is St. Therese, one who truly cares and who intercedes on our behalf.   —*Joy, Montana*

Chapter 3

PEACE

The Lord will give strength to His people;
the Lord will bless His people with peace.

—Psalm 29:11

The Miracle of Reconciliation

For some time, in the spring of 1997, I had been praying fervently to God. I had asked Our Lady to please
intercede on my behalf for a favor that I urgently requested, provided that it was no obstacle to my salvation.
The nature of the request and how I came to need it are
unimportant. What was important was being made one with
the Body of Christ again, and I am convinced that many of
the struggles I endured were no doubt part of making that
happen.

Despite my most urgent pleading, I got the sense that
Our Lady couldn't fully help me, given the mortal state of
disgrace that I was in. I got distracted on so many occasions
while praying my daily Rosary that I knew I had to fix this
situation before I could receive the graces for which I was
praying.

It was at this point that I committed myself to making an
act of Reconciliation, and determined to consecrate myself
to Mary's Immaculate Heart. I had finally realized that I
could no longer do this alone. I had tried it my way and, as
in all cases of human arrogance, failed. Stubborn to the end,
however, I wanted to know at least one thing from God — I
wanted to know that my prayers were being heard. I would
leave the final decision to Him, of course, in His eternal
wisdom.

That is when I came across the little pamphlet about
St. Therese of Lisieux that I had picked up in church some
time before. I read the story of Father Putigan and his
Novena of the twenty-four Glory Be's to St. Therese of the
Child Jesus.

Calling upon St. Therese to pray for me with Our Lady, to whom she is so precious, and to Our Lord, I began the novena. I was emboldened by Father Putigan's successful request that as a sign his novena was being heard St. Therese would send him a flower. Therefore, I asked the Little Flower to also send me a rose, to know that Our Father was hearing my pleas.

For nine days I said the novena, and for nine days nothing happened. I still had not made a confession, and I still had not consecrated myself to the Immaculate Heart. The next day, June 7, was the feast of the Immaculate Heart of Mary and a First Saturday, no less. I took my daughter, not quite seven years old, to the Basilica of the National Shrine of the Immaculate Conception. Here, I made a very long and complete confession and was relieved once again that I could now enjoy the blessing of the Holy Eucharist.

I could not resist the urgings of my little girl that she too be allowed to make her First Confession at the same time. Since she knew all the prayers and I believed was fully conscious of what she felt she had done wrong, I relented, making the day even more of a special occasion.

Since the hour was late, we missed the First Saturday devotion to Our Lady in the Chapel of the Immaculate Heart. I still wanted to go there to make my consecration, however, and decided that doing so in private would be perfect. On the way, a woman stopped me to comment how wonderful she thought it was that I was taking my daughter to confession with me and what a wonderful, fatherly example I was setting. Given what I had just told God, I certainly didn't feel like much of a role model. However, it was undeniable how thoroughly my daughter enjoyed the experience. I told the woman how proud I was of her and told her what we were planning to do next. The woman turned to my daughter and asked her if she might like to have something from our Blessed Mother. She didn't have to ask twice.

We walked into the Chapel of the Immaculate Heart and, there at the front, was the Pilgrim Virgin Statue of Our Lady of Fatima. As we approached the statue, the woman asked my daughter to pick from some of the many flowers that surrounded the statue as a souvenir of this memorable day. Only if the Blessed Mother herself had given my daughter these flowers could she have felt more honored. After carefully selecting a small bouquet, we thanked the lady, who asked us to pray for her as she turned to leave.

Smiling, I asked my daughter to say a "Hail Mary" for the kind woman, which she did, and one for herself, and to sit for a moment while I made my consecration. I approached the altar next to the statue. Mustering all the commitment I could, I gave myself completely to Our Heavenly Mother, asking her to always lead me to her Son, as I committed to imitating her virtues. As I knelt on the marble, my only wish was that, like the children at Fatima, I could make my consecration in the Blessed Virgin's physical presence.

When I had finished, I stood up and told my daughter, who had watched closely, that we should be going now. Together we walked out of the chapel, and I thought how perfect this day had been, how close I felt to Christ, to Our Lady...and to my little girl. I relished the fact that now I could pray, cleansed from all stain of sin, for Our Lord's grace.

Looking up at me with her big green eyes, my daughter extended her flowers toward me and asked, "Daddy, could you hold these? You can have one." I walked only a few paces before breaking down into tears. It suddenly occurred to me that on the day after my novena, minutes after I had been reunited with God and only seconds after standing with contrite heart before His Mother and consecrating myself to her Immaculate Heart, I received my sign. St. Therese, that most beloved saint, had fulfilled my wish — with a rose from the Mother of God, no less! Heaven had only been waiting for me to open my heart.

Concerned at my tears, my little girl wanted to know what was wrong. We sat down so I could explain what had just happened. As if the point had not been driven home clear enough, she looked at me and said something I had never heard her say: "Miracles come from prayer, Daddy."

St. Therese of the Child Jesus, pray for us!

— *Michael, Virginia*

The Photograph

Last summer, my college-age daughter, Lauren, attended World Youth Day in Toronto with our parish youth group. On one of the days, she visited the Shrine of St. Therese the Little Flower in Detroit. In the garden there, she noticed a pink rose so beautiful she felt compelled to take a photo of it. Lauren has no special interest or training in photography and was using an ordinary instamatic camera. At first the camera would not snap the picture. Lauren kept trying to press the button, but the camera would not cooperate. Just as she was about to give up, the camera went "click" and snapped the photo.

As soon as Lauren arrived home, she had the film developed at the local pharmacy. When she brought the photos

*Photograph brings
peace and healing*

home, we all looked through them with her. Since the pharmacy offered doubles of each picture at a nominal cost,
Lauren had two sets of prints made. As we looked through
the photos, we stopped to wonder at the beauty of the picture of the rose. It was exquisite, an opening bud with dew
clinging to it. The lighting and shadows made the photo very
dramatic and beautiful. Lauren laughed as she told us of the
difficulty she had in taking the shot. We were amazed. The
picture of the rose looked like a professional had taken it.

A few days later, Lauren was talking on the phone with
a friend from college. She learned that another friend from
school, Jenny, had lost her mother to cancer about a week

earlier. Lauren felt very sad for Jenny and tried unsuccessfully to reach her friend by phone. Still wanting to comfort her, Lauren prayed for Jenny and her family and then wrote a lovely note to her. On impulse, Lauren decided to include a copy of the rose photo.

A short time after, the girls returned to Notre Dame for the fall term. Jenny was anxious to visit Lauren because she had a special story to share. On the day before Lauren's letter arrived, Jenny and her sister had taken on the sad task of sorting through some of their mother's personal belongings in order to spare their grieving father this pain. As she looked through her mother's purse, Jenny came across a holy card of St. Therese holding a bouquet of pink roses. The back of the card explained the novena and promise of a rose. Jenny's mother and grandmother shared a great devotion to the Little Flower, but Jenny had never paid much attention to the Saint. At that moment, though, Jenny decided to reach out to St. Therese for help. She asked for a sign that her mother was all right. She told St. Therese that she did not want to wait for nine days, that she needed help sooner. She asked her to send the sign the next day.

Well, as you may have already guessed, Lauren's letter and the beautiful photo arrived the very next day. Jenny was utterly shocked as she opened the envelope and found the picture. She knew right away that her prayers had been answered because the rose in the photograph looked exactly like the roses in St. Therese's bouquet. When she held the picture next to the prayer card, she was amazed at how identical the images were. Jenny called her grandmother immediately and shared the story and the photo with her mother's grieving mother. She told Lauren that the worst of her grief stopped immediately on that day. Now, more than a year later, both Jenny and her grandmother remain at peace thanks to the intercession of the Little Flower and her sign of the rose.   — *Nancy, Minneapolis*

A Flower by Any Other Name

I've always loved the saints, but I was not particularly drawn to St. Therese of Lisieux. She seemed far too popular for me to establish a relationship with her. Based on the huge following she had, I guess I figured she had her hands full with intercessions. But surprisingly enough — and I have no doubt about this — she has reached out to me on more than one occasion.

I consider myself a devout Catholic. I went to Catholic grade school, graduated from a Catholic college, was married in a Catholic church, attend Mass every weekend, and raised my children in the Catholic faith. It wasn't until my health became threatened, however, that my Catholic faith was really put to the test.

After the birth of my third daughter, I suffered a miscarriage. It was an ectopic pregnancy that resulted in emergency surgery. The years following this loss took their toll on my husband and me both emotionally and physically. On top of this, my mother-in-law, whom I loved dearly, died after a short battle with cancer. This caused my grieving husband to become very distant. To make matters worse, I developed what is known as adenomyosis, resulting in excessive bleeding and constant pain due to the deterioration of the uterine wall.

Between the loss of our fourth child and the loss of a parent, my marriage was under the most stress it had ever endured. Neither of us would talk about it. My physical condition worsened, and I was diagnosed with precancerous cells on my cervix. Despite several surgeries to remove these cells, they continued to grow back more aggressively. At this time, my doctor gave us the grim news that I would most likely not be able to carry any more children to term. In fact, he was advising me to have a radical hysterectomy. In the meantime, I was trying every type of prescription medication to control the physical symptoms, hoping that perhaps one would work and I could have another child. Desperate, I began attending a weekly prayer group at my parish. It was there that I first learned of the novena of St. Therese, the "Little Flower."

One day when I was at the local pharmacy waiting for yet another ineffective prescription to be filled, I came so close to fainting I had to get down on my knees and place my head on a low shelf. My pharmacist gently suggested I go ahead and have the surgery. She knew I had tried every medication available to treat my condition. In my heart, I knew she was right.

The week before my scheduled surgery, I started the novena to St. Therese. I prayed for God's will to be done. If He wished for me to be cured and have more children, then so be it. If He wished for me to have a radical hysterectomy and serve Him in other ways, fine. I just wanted some peace in the matter. I prayed faithfully every day, but I also informed St. Therese in no uncertain terms that I thought the "shower of roses" deal claimed by the women in the prayer group was a bunch of baloney, and she could save her flowers. I didn't like roses anyway; my favorite flowers are daisies.

As the days passed, I grew weaker. Although I was very dizzy and had to fight just to stand upright, I really wanted to attend Sunday Mass before my scheduled surgery. I didn't want anyone to know of my pain, so I prayed to St. Therese to help me through this one Mass. To be honest, by this time I had lost track of the days of the novena. I was just praying it. At the closing song, when I opened the hymnal I had been using all through Mass, I found tucked in the pages a patch, like you sew on clothes. Of all things, it was an orange daisy patch! I gasped and sat down suddenly. The friend I was with, thinking I was feeling bad, questioned if I was okay. I was shaking like a leaf. St. Therese had helped me through Mass, as I'd asked, and even sent me a flower to let me know she had heard my prayers. Not any flower, mind you, but a *daisy*, my favorite flower! I quickly counted the days and, sure enough, it was the ninth day of the novena.

The next day, I entered my surgery with complete peace. My husband was amazed. The surgery went fine, and my health returned. I shared this story with him, and it has become an important part of our healing. We are now celebrating our seventeenth wedding anniversary together with much happiness and a renewed appreciation for our three healthy and beautiful daughters.

The clincher to this story, however, happened when my husband and I were on a young adults' pilgrimage in Europe and we had the opportunity to spend a day in Lisieux, France. After the tour of St. Therese's family home, the Carmelite convent, and the beautiful basilica, we boarded our tour bus. The tour guide shared a little known story about St. Therese. She told us that the Saint's favorite flower was not a rose as most people assumed; it was actually... a daisy.

I wanted to melt right there. St. Therese is such a special saint and has the most wonderful ways of touching even stubborn hearts like mine! She has without question worked her way into my life, and I consider her a cherished friend.

— *Colleen, New York*

Emotional Turmoil

I grew up in a Catholic family where my father, Thaddeus (whom everyone called Ted), had a special devotion to St. Therese of Lisieux. Whenever a crisis occurred — a problem, an illness, or a loss — he would tell us that he was going to pray to St. Therese because she always listened and interceded. He actually credited the Saint with helping him get through World War II. I was a typical kid at the time, and though I heard my father talk about St. Therese repeatedly, I never really took it to heart.

It wasn't until years later as an adult that I came to understand what my dad had experienced. Within a three-year period, several terrible events occurred in my life. My father, suffering from diabetic neuropathy, became bedfast. I had major back surgery that forced me to spend four months flat on my back in recovery. My mother, the caregiver for both of us, was stressed and exhausted. I eventually returned to work only to find that my company was downsizing and it was just a matter of time before I would lose my job of twenty-four years. Here I was, middle-aged and faced with starting my career over again, so I enrolled in college. During my first week of classes, my father passed away. To make matters worse, my long-time boyfriend, Ron, was diagnosed with cirrhosis of the liver.

Although I attended Mass regularly, I felt I needed something more to see me through this emotional turmoil. I decided to begin a novena. I chose to invoke the intercession of St. Therese, recalling the many times my dad said she had helped him. Maybe she could help me, too.

During this time, a very strange thing happened. Ron and I went to the mall for no reason in particular. We were walking around my favorite department store, chatting, and not really paying attention to where we were going. We wound up in the accessories department. Suddenly, I was drawn like a magnet to what appeared to be some sort of a pamphlet trimmed in gold and sticking up between a display of wallets. I picked it up to discover that it was a beautiful St. Therese prayer card. I had never seen one like this before. My first thought was how unusual it was for this card to be here of all places. Could this be a sign from the Saint that she had heard my prayer? The thought of it made me shake. I also knew that I couldn't just leave the card there — surely, it was meant for me. I selected a pair of socks and brought the card and the socks to the cash register. The clerk simply rang up the socks and bagged them with the card without comment. Shortly after, Ron bought me a beautiful St. Therese medal, which my pastor blessed for me. Wearing the medal and saying the novena daily, I became very connected to St. Therese.

Ron had also been raised Catholic. However, he had fallen away from the Church for a few years. It was only during our relationship that he returned, which made me very happy. Although he was not a member of my parish, Ron attended Mass and received Holy Communion with me there regularly. Each time we heard the song "Be Not Afraid," he would remind me that this was his favorite hymn. I gave Ron a copy of the St. Therese prayer card to help him cope with his illness. He continued to attend Mass until the progression of the cirrhosis became unbearable and he was hospitalized. He passed away at the young age of forty-seven, three months prior to my college graduation.

His death was a horrible shock for me and left me feeling very distraught. Through it all, I continued my novena. Ron's family took charge of the funeral arrangements. I received a phone call from his sister, who informed me that because Ron wasn't registered at a parish, he would not be able to have a priest or a Catholic funeral Mass. I was very angry and told her adamantly that this was unacceptable. Ron had been attending Mass and receiving Holy Communion every Sunday! Surely there was a priest somewhere that would offer a funeral Mass for him. His sister's aloof attitude greatly disturbed me. Feeling helpless, I turned that night to St. Therese.

Early the next morning, Ron's sister called again. In a cheerful voice she told me that the family had located a priest and a parish and that everything was properly arranged for Ron. I can still remember that tremendous feeling of relief—I was so grateful. My prayers were answered. When I inquired about the name of the church in which Ron's Mass would be celebrated, I was told, "St. Therese's." I was overcome.

I arrived at the funeral home early so I could have some time by myself with Ron. When the priest walked in, I was so elated to see him that I broke down in tears. He was a wonderful priest and his consoling words left me feeling extremely comforted. After talking with him for a while, it occurred to me that I didn't even know his name. When I asked, he replied, "I have an unusual name. My name is

Thaddeus, but you can call me Ted." I was speechless. That was my father's name!

With mixed feelings of sadness and peace, I arrived at the church to hear the organist play the most appropriate entrance hymn: "Be Not Afraid." I knew then and there that everything was going to be okay. Trying to control my emotions, I slid into a pew and looked up only to see directly in front of me the smiling statue of St. Therese. The entire day was completely overwhelming.

Ron was buried at a cemetery that is approximately a one-hour drive from my home. A few months later, I returned to visit the gravesite. I noticed that a headstone, which was selected by his family, was now in place. As I approached it slowly, I noticed to my utter astonishment that it was etched with a beautiful picture of St. Therese.

Today I continue to pray the novena that I found at the department store. I have obtained additional copies and have shared them with many people, including non-Catholics. I have also read several books about St. Therese's life, and I feel like I know her very well. I pray that Ron will introduce me to this wonderful saint one day when we all meet in heaven.   — *Mary Jane, Pennsylvania*

Petals of Peace

In November 1991, my thirty-three-year-old nephew, Anthony, was diagnosed with cancer. I immediately became resolved that he would fully recover and that I would help him. I sent him names of the best doctors (which he already had), articles, books, tapes, and Mass cards. I spent hours reading about his type of cancer, always searching for the book that offered the most optimistic view.

More hours were spent as I imaged the cancer cells leaving his body when he underwent chemotherapy. My daily Masses and Rosaries were said for him alone, and I had to alternate the saints to whom I prayed — there were so many.

Most days, I functioned with a heavy heart as I rode alongside Anthony on the roller coaster ride of remissions and recurrences, and watched this tall, handsome young man patiently suffer with this hellish disease. I even joined a family member cancer support group.

In December 1993, less than two weeks after my nephew's third surgery, his mother (my sister) died quite suddenly. I believe she died of a broken heart. Emotionally, I was at rock bottom, and, physically, I suffered from a stress-related chronic illness that recurred intermittently.

The following April, Anthony was in extremely critical condition after more chemotherapy and a fourth operation. He miraculously survived, even going back to work. At this point, I believe the Lord, who knew how poorly I was coping, sent St. Therese to help me. I received a strong inspiration to pray to her daily. I began to implore her intercession for my nephew's cure and asked her to send me roses if my prayer request was granted. Coincidentally, Anthony was born on October 1, St. Therese's feast day.

Between April 23, 1994, and June 13, 1995, I had twenty-nine rose encounters, most in the form of rose petals on the streets of Manhattan. Some were quite impressive. On busy West Fifty-seventh Street, I found two large red rose petals. While attending a music festival in the mountains, I found more petals adhered to the base of a water fountain. I even saw three fresh tea rose petals lined up perfectly on a city sidewalk in the month of December. My only concern with these frequent sightings was that often the rose petals appeared to be crushed.

Still, my heart was lighter and I was filled with some hope. Despite this, Anthony was not being cured. In fact, he had a fifth operation in September 1994. For the first time, it seemed easier for me to accept the thought of my nephew's possible death than it had ever been before. Was I experiencing false hope with these signs of roses while the whole time God was working on my ability to become more accepting of His will? I scolded St. Therese — after all, there were to be no roses unless Anthony was cured. The petals stopped appearing for a while, and then they started again.

On June 4, 1995, I made my annual visit to St. Anthony's Festival. Kneeling before the Saint's statue, I begged this miracle worker to intercede for my nephew, his namesake. Later, walking home, I found a rose petal. Five days later, I found another one, only hours before Anthony died.

St. Anthony of Padua left this world on Friday, June 13, 1231, at the age of thirty-six. On Tuesday, June 17, 1231, many miracles occurred at his gravesite.

My nephew, Anthony, left this world on Friday, June 9, 1995, also at the age of thirty-six. On Tuesday, June 13, 1995, I believe two extraordinary saints gave a spectacular performance.

That morning, after my prayers to St. Anthony, I asked St. Therese to send me a rose if Anthony's soul was in heaven or on its way there. Later, as I approached my church rectory to arrange a memorial Mass, I found at the bottom of the steps one quite dry but very significant long-stemmed white rose.

It's a rare soul that needs no purification before entering heaven. Perhaps my nephew spent a brief time in purgatory and on Tuesday, June 13, St. Therese gathered her rose petals to create a path while St. Anthony came to meet his namesake to lead him into the Eternal Light.

— *Lucille, New York*

The Retreat

It began as a little thing, unplanned on my part and not amounting to much, as things of import often do. A friend called to invite me on a one-day retreat a couple of hours from home. I said, "Yes!" immediately, as I was happy to escape, even if only briefly, the havoc my husband was wreaking on our household at the time.

The retreat, as it turned out, was held in Darien, Illinois, at the National Shrine of St. Therese of Lisieux. It was led by a Carmelite, although the retreat itself had nothing to do with Therese. My friend suggested we tour the Shrine since we were there anyway. I was agreeable, although as a non-Catholic I knew little about this saint. In fact, the only reason I was even familiar with her name was that my daughter, whom we raised Catholic, chose Therese as her Confirmation name.

The retreat was a refreshing day in an interesting place, an oasis in the vast and barren desert of my life. But the tour of the Shrine itself turned out to have an even greater impact on me, touching me in a very special and unexpected way. I remember vividly the stunning stained-glass characters and scenes in the chapel windows, the incredible wood carving depiction of the events in Therese's life, the interesting stories and artifacts, relics and photographs, as well as the little chair from Therese's tiny cell in the convent of Lisieux. This experience marked the beginning of my curiosity regarding the Little Flower's life and what it could possibly have to do with my own.

My next encounter with Therese took place three months later, when I finally made the difficult and emotional decision to leave my unfaithful husband and take up residence at the Shalom Retreat Center in Dubuque, Iowa. The center's director, Sister Marie-Therese, recognized my bewildered, exhausted state and offered me refuge for a period of three months. Once again, I had found an oasis. She also graciously offered to let me participate in any of the directed retreats that would be taking place during my stay.

Eager to find peace and healing, I happened into the first one available — a three-day retreat on *St. Therese of Lisieux*. The more I learned of Therese's story and spirituality, the more fascinated I became. She and I had "little conversations" on my walks around the retreat grounds. I sensed her presence in my own small cell, and I had the feeling that I knew her. It was like I'd *always* known her. But how could this be possible?

My interest in and affection for Therese continued to grow. At one point, I revisited the Shrine to ask, "What is this about? Dear Therese, Little Flower, who *are* you to me?" I kept expecting something major to happen, but it never did. It didn't take long for me to realize that Therese was drawing me not to herself, but to her "little way," that through it, I might know Jesus.

At the end of my stay at Shalom, I had an opportunity to make a twelve-day journaling retreat with Joseph F. Schmidt, author of *Praying with Therese of Lisieux* (St. Mary's Press, 1995), whom I came to think of fondly as "St. Joe." Brother Joseph is a Franciscan and a great devotee and student of St. Therese. Though the retreat was offered for religious, I was allowed to participate.

During these intense twelve days, I entered into a process of giving up the great effort that had become my life. I realized that up until that point, I had spent all my energy *striving*. I was always striving for something: to raise a family perfectly, to please other people, to do the right thing, to control the outcome of situations, and, above all, to please God. All of this outward effort had consumed me until there was nothing left. Although the retreat involved a tremendous amount of pain, especially regarding the brutality I suffered in my marriage, it opened the door to healing. Through the example of Therese, I gained the strength I needed to act for myself and take the necessary steps forward. Therese showed me how to cooperate with God's love for me, to trust in His grace, and to be willing to take small but critical steps. This incredible retreat experience allowed me to finally arrive at a place where I knew for certain that God loved me no matter what, whether I pleased Him or anyone else. I, who for so long strove to attain perfection, heard Therese's gentle wisdom in these words: "Perfection seems simple to me; I see it is sufficient to recognize one's nothingness and to abandon oneself as a child into God's arms."

My friendship with Therese also heralded the beginning of my interest in the Catholic Church. I believe my conversion to Catholicism had much to do with the intercession of Our Blessed Mother, the apologetics of Dr. Scott Hahn, and the writings of several Catholic authors. When I was ready to formally enter the Church, the time came for me to choose a Confirmation name. I called my daughter and asked, "How do you choose a saint?" Her response was something Therese herself might have said. "You don't choose a saint, Mom," my daughter wisely pointed out. "Saints choose you!"

— *Deborah, Minnesota*

Life after Death

My mother and I were very close, so close that it is hard to explain in words the wonderful relationship I had with her. She had breast cancer and, after a thirteen-year battle, passed away on September 20, 2001.

When October 1 came along, I invited a friend of mine to a Mass in honor of the Little Flower at the Carmelite Monastery in Latrobe. She, too, has a special fondness for the Little Flower, and I thought she might enjoy being at the monastery and celebrating the feast of St. Therese.

We arrived at the monastery and, as I knelt down in prayer, I offered my Mass for my mother, that she would be happy in heaven. I just wanted her to be at peace. It was a beautiful Mass, at the end of which the Carmelite sisters distributed blessed roses, and we all went home.

The next day was a beautiful October day. I decided I should put my porch furniture away for the winter, knowing we would not have many more nice days like this one. I carried the furniture, piece by piece, into the garage until I was finished.

In order to understand what happened next, I have to mention that my mother had given me a climbing rose bush that grew beautifully, year after year, until this last year. Therefore, in early spring, I asked my husband to cut off all the dead branches and throw them away in the hopes that the plant would grow better. My husband did as I asked, but I never realized that instead of throwing the dead branches away, he tossed them in a pile just outside of the garage. I supposed I had been too caught up in caring for my very sick mother to notice them.

On my last trip out of the garage after putting the porch furniture away, I spotted in the corner of my eye something small and colorful. Looking down, I saw the dead branches, brown and leafless, yet from one of these branches emerged a red rose in full bloom. I knew then that St. Therese had given me a sign that my mom was happy with our dear Lord. It was a sign of God's promise of life after death.

— *Phyllis, Pennsylvania*

A Perfect Cascade

This story is true and not directed to any specific people, church, or belief but is written for everyone. When my son, Dennis, was to be operated on for a tumor on his skull, a complication of renal cell cancer, I was not dealing with it too well. He had already had a kidney removed prior to this, and my emotions were not fully recovered from that experience.

A good friend gave me a prayer card and suggested I pray to St. Therese of the Child Jesus and the Holy Face. Before her death at a very young age, St. Therese promised to spend her heaven sending a shower of roses from the heavenly garden to the souls on earth, to bring them to God. I turned to this saint and prayed most fervently that she take my request to God for my son to have a successful surgery.

The day of the operation, several family members joined me at the hospital. The waiting room outside of the OR was too crowded, so they directed us to another one on another floor. It too, was a bit crowded at first, but began to empty as lunchtime approached. I was too distraught to leave and welcomed the time to myself. I was not alone long when a Roman Catholic priest came in and sat down across from me. I felt a strong urge to talk to him, and asked if he would please pray with me for my son. He took my hand and we prayed together. I was greatly comforted.

When the priest got up to leave, I asked him his name. "Father Rose," he replied. I couldn't believe my ears. I told him excitedly about praying for St. Therese to send me a rose as a message of love and confirmation. "My dear," replied the priest. "You have been praying for a rose, and here I am. Alphonse Rose." Dennis came through the surgery just fine. Although he died two years later, I am convinced those extra years of life were courtesy of the intercession of St. Therese.

I was blessed with another miracle more recently. I had suffered from two strokes that produced damage in both the right and left sides of my brain. After three weeks of hospitalization and rehab, it was determined that my vision was severely impaired to the point where I cannot read, drive a car, or walk without the assistance of a walker. Again, I went to St. Therese in prayer and asked her to send me a shower of roses and to ask God, if it is His will, to restore my vision.

Several days later, a literal shower of fragrant pink roses appeared over my back fence. The vine was meandering through a mulberry tree in the adjacent yard, with the roses spilling into my property in a perfect cascade. From the lounge chair to which I am confined, the roses are in direct line of my weakened vision. They cannot be seen from my neighbor's yard, or from any other location in my own house. When my friends and relatives came over for further inspection, they could not discover the source of this mysterious plant. No one had ever seen anything like it.

Some of my friends urged me to pick at least one of the roses as a memento, but I refused. I felt they were too holy. For two weeks, I enjoyed their beauty. Then, suddenly, they were gone. The neighbors and the young man who cares for my yard could find no trace of them. There were no dried or dead buds, no sign of a vine. Nothing.

Although I am still hoping for a change in my medical condition, my interpretation of St. Therese's message is that God has heard my petition and will answer in His own way and time. No matter how or when He answers, I am at peace and in complete accord with Him. I only pray that this literal shower of roses will help bring souls on earth to God. As for me, I will walk on whatever path He leads me and accept whatever He asks of me obediently and willingly with thanksgiving that He does indeed love His children and hears their prayers. — *Claire, Maryland*

Family Forgiveness

I used to tell God that if He ever answered this prayer, I would consider it a miracle. We have two children, a boy named Simon and a girl named Carly. There are nine years between them and something went terribly wrong when Carly was five, something so horribly unspeakable, it changed our lives for ten long years.

When Carly was thirteen, she confessed to me that her brother had molested her for years, swearing her to complete secrecy. This shocking news threw our family into an upheaval of overwhelming pain and misery. It literally tore us apart. Carly mournfully revealed how deeply this situation had affected her mind, how she suffered flashbacks and relived the torture every time she looked at her brother. She told me for years she tried to block out the whole experience, but to no avail. It particularly came to a head one day after Simon had been away for six months, and his sudden return made the memories come flooding back to her to the point where she could no longer bear it.

Devastated for my daughter and my family, I made arrangements for Carly to see a counselor. She refused to allow her brother to attend the sessions, as she could not face him. Before long, she stopped going altogether — the memories were just too painful.

One night, after Simon had been at the house, I went into Carly's room to check on her. When I opened the door I could tell by the look on her face we were in trouble. We took her to the hospital and had her admitted under a suicide watch. A week later, Carly returned home with an appointment to see a psychiatrist. She was found to be suffering from Post Traumatic Stress and a dissociative disorder in which she suffered from multiple personalities, only in her case they were all her own personalities at different ages.

At this time, Carly had started living at school, and she eventually refused to go to any more therapy sessions. Then, late one night, we got a call from our daughter that she was planning to die. Fortunately, we got to her in time and again she was hospitalized. This time, she dropped out of school and came home to live with us. We could not allow Simon to come home while Carly was there. For ten years he did not come home for Christmas or even call on the phone for fear she might answer. We had to go to him. Mind you, my son was living in the same hell as the rest of us. He was so sorry for what had happened and wanted to heal with his sister, but Carly was not ready or able to forgive her brother. She even called him from time to time, threatening to call the police and have him put in jail. Our family lived in complete and utter misery during this time with no hope of ever escaping this nightmare. No matter how much I prayed for peace and forgiveness to heal our family, the situation remained the same.

Just about the time I was reaching my breaking point, the reliquary of St. Therese was passing through town. My son, through an unusual turn of events, became the driver for the "Theresemobile." He spent three days driving the sacred relics from church to church, and all the time he was with this holy saint he begged for her intercession.

Three weeks later, Carly saw her brother driving on the street and mentioned it to me in passing. This may not seem miraculous to an outsider, but bear in mind Carly had not mentioned Simon's name once in ten years. (She even for a while, when asked if she had siblings, told people she was an only child.) I told my daughter that Simon had seen her as well, but didn't want to upset her by waving. What Carly said next shocked me so profoundly I thought I might faint on the spot. She said matter-of-factly that she wasn't angry anymore, it just wasn't worth it, and to tell Simon the next time to wave. Only a month before, she had made one of her threatening phone calls to him!

Relics tour the United States, October 1999–January 2000
Photo credit: Rita K. Tinetti

A few more weeks passed by. Carly and I were at a local hospital to visit someone. Just as we were about to enter the room, Simon walked out. There they stood, brother and sister, face-to-face for the first time in years. I was so scared I couldn't even breathe. Carly told Simon that things were okay, that she was feeling good. I thought I was dreaming. It was truly the miracle I had been seeking.

I am confident that St. Therese had interceded for my daughter and that God graced Carly with the power to forgive. It still brings tears to my eyes whenever I think about that moment. Carly told me later that for years she had out-of-body experiences, which is common with her disorder. She said one day (shortly after her brother had started praying to St. Therese) that she felt all the other parts of her personalities become one. She was so frightened she started crying because she didn't know what was happening. Now we all recognize this as a miraculous healing.

Just so we would never doubt St. Therese's involvement in this matter, we received the proverbial sign of roses. I had asked Simon to get me some of the roses from the reliquary, which he did. I had planned to keep some of the petals and give the rest to my mother. I carefully placed the rose petals in an envelope to save. A few months passed and I forgot all about the petals until my husband went to give Carly something in an envelope. When she opened it, she asked, "What's with all the rose petals?" I looked and realized that it was the same envelope I used to save the petals. I have no recollection of putting that envelope back in the box. To me, it was St. Therese sending roses from her reliquary that were delivered from my son's hands into my daughter's. It was the ultimate sign of forgiveness.

Today, my children are on very good terms and my daughter is mentally healthy, happily married, and expecting her first child. She is thinking of making her brother the godfather. My children together bought me a three-foot statue of St. Therese, which is one of my greatest treasures. Without this dear saint's intercession and the power of forgiveness, nothing would have ever changed in our family. I am truly blessed. Thank you, St. Therese of Lisieux.   —*Anonymous*

Grief Turned to Joy

I live in La Vista, Nebraska, which is a suburb of Omaha. Some friends told me about St. Therese's relics coming to Sioux City, Iowa, on November 8, 1999, at the Discalced Carmelite Monastery. Sioux City is about a two-hour drive from Omaha. Mount Michael Abbey, in

Elkhorn, Nebraska, had scheduled a pilgrimage for anyone who would like to go to see the relics. I signed up immediately. St. Therese is my patron saint, and the opportunity to see her relics was something I just couldn't miss.

A few days before the pilgrimage, I woke up to very disturbing news. Five of my former co-workers and friends at Xerox in Honolulu (where I had worked for three and a half years before moving to Nebraska) were killed by another co-worker. I was close to these fine men when I worked with them and became friends with their families as well. One was like a brother to me, and his wife was like a sister. We had still kept in touch over the years, even sending Christmas gifts to one another.

So it was with a heavy heart that I went to view St. Therese's relics. Of course, as expected, the church and grounds were packed with other pilgrims. My group was led downstairs to the basement to watch the Mass on a television that was set up so we could see what was going on above us.

It was very tough to hear the Mass because of the machinery in the boiler room, which made loud noises from time to time. I sat and participated in the Mass, as best I could, and then asked St. Therese during a quiet time in the liturgy to please ask Jesus to take care of my friends who had died, to take care of their families, and to forgive the one who had killed them.

About ten minutes later, I began to notice the distinct smell of roses. It was very faint at first, and then, in waves, it grew stronger and stronger. I wondered if it had to do with something going on upstairs. Finally, I turned to my friend's sister, sitting next to me, and asked if she could smell the fragrance of roses. She just looked at me strangely for a moment, and then her expression changed and she said that she could. She turned to ask her mom, who was sitting next to her, if she smelled roses, and after a bit she replied that she could, as well. We all smiled at one another and said nothing else.

The subject didn't get brought up again until we were on the way back home on the bus. The priest who had accompanied us, Father Daniel, was walking around the bus asking all of us if we experienced anything out of the ordinary. He stood by my seat for the longest time talking to everyone and kept looking at me, but for some reason I could not tell him what had happened. It felt like I wasn't supposed to discuss it at that time. No one else on the bus mentioned that they had smelled the fragrance of roses.

Later, my friend confessed that she had told Father Daniel about my experience. She also said that before I had said anything to her about the wonderful fragrance of roses, she hadn't noticed anything. Once I had asked her about it, the fragrance became stronger and stronger, and then it was gone as quickly as it appeared.

I am sure that the fragrance of roses was sent from St. Therese as an answer to my prayers. I know she interceded for me to Jesus. I left the Mass discovering that the incredible grief I had experienced earlier was now replaced with a profound sense of peace. I felt wonderful for having the opportunity to be there in the first place, and I now basked in indescribable joy!

In her autobiography, *Story of a Soul*, St. Therese recounted a spiritual experience that she kept to herself for a while before relating it to someone. Once she shared it, she felt its magnitude diminish. Sometimes it seems these little blessings that are given to us are meant for us to hold on to for a while or maybe they are simply meant just for us. Now, however, I feel it is time to share this experience with others in the hopes that it might bring someone else peace and joy.   — *Theresa "Carol," Nebraska*

A Peaceful Passing

My mother, Maud, passed away on January 2, 2003, at the age of ninety-three. She spent her last four years as a resident of the Carmel Richmond Rehabilitation and Nursing Home in Staten Island, New York.

Getting my mother into Carmel had not been easy. I prayed hard and often to St. Therese of Lisieux for years that a room would open for her. Carmel was such a wonderful nursing home and the atmosphere was warm and kind. Mom was put on the waiting list, and I was told to call every Wednesday to see if a room became available for her. Week after week, the answer was always no. After a year, I gave up calling weekly but still prayed that St. Therese would answer my prayers. Then, the call came. Carmel had a bed available. Eagerly, I accepted it.

My only regret was that Mom couldn't really appreciate what a beautiful new nursing home she was going to, although I think when she saw the Carmelite nuns it seemed to trigger fond memories in her. Some days Mom was kind of with it, but most days, she wasn't. She was wheelchair-bound and pretty soon could no longer feed herself. Some days she knew me, most of the time she didn't, but we could sort of speak with our eyes at times. I loved her so.

In early January, I got the phone call from Carmel to come right down. I knew her time was near since Mom was having trouble with the nasal feeding tube. When I arrived that afternoon, one of the Carmelites was sitting in a corner praying the Rosary. It is a policy of the sisters that when a resident is near the end, one of them will stay until the family comes so they will not pass alone.

I sat beside my mother with my St. Therese chaplet. I stroked her hand while I prayed my chaplet, imploring that Mom would go quietly and not be afraid. I prayed that the Lord would gently take her hand and lead her home (a song that we loved). My daughter soon joined me, stroking my mother's forehead and other hand, both of us praying to St. Therese to hear our prayer and take her quietly so she wouldn't be afraid.

As time passed and I was deep in prayer, I heard my daughter say, "Mom, I think she's going." I looked up and, with a soft sigh, my mother was gone. It was 11:25 p.m. I didn't know anyone could go so peacefully, and I thanked St. Therese immediately.

The nurses kindly asked us to leave the room so they could straighten up. My daughter and I went down to the chapel and said a few more prayers. After a while, we returned to my mother's room. Just before we reached her door, we were greeted with a very strong smell. My daughter said it smelled like roses. "Who would bring roses up here this late at night?" I wondered. My daughter suggested that perhaps the nurses sprayed rose water or powder on Grandma or in her room.

We entered Mom's room, kissed her goodnight, and left with heavy hearts. It wasn't until we got home and sat down with a cup of tea, reviewing the events of the evening, that it suddenly hit us. The heavy smell of roses — St. Therese had been there!

The next day, when I related what had happened to the sisters, one of them said that St. Therese must have heard our prayers, come down from heaven, and took Mom by the hand to lead her home. Neither my daughter nor I will ever forget the pungent smell of roses outside my mother's room, or the absolute peace we felt in our hearts. Mom died on January 2, the birthday of St. Therese, the Little Flower. Coincidence?

— *Leota, New York*

Wild Roses

I am still in awe about a favor I recently received from St. Therese of Lisieux. My fiancé had reached what seemed like rock bottom with his drinking. I felt the whole situation — and our future — was a lost cause. Defeated, I could no longer stand by and watch what I felt was certain death for him.

I left my fiancé and returned to my home more than eight hundred miles away, clutching my Rosary the entire trip. The pain in my heart was so heavy, I begged Jesus to please help me. I arrived home and opened up the windows to get some relief from the muggy heat of summer. To my surprise, I had an immediate visitor.

A fifty-seven-year-old woman from our small country village, who was known to have some sort of emotional problem, walked in unannounced. In her arms was a stem of wild roses with two full pink flowers and three small buds on the branches. Without a word, she handed it to me. I accepted this strange gift, placed the stem in a glass of water, and set up tea for the two of us.

After the woman had left, I pulled out a box that had been tucked under the coffee table and began to look through my back mail. As I did so, a card with a novena prayer to St. Therese fell onto the floor, not far from the rose branch I had been given.

I stared at the image of St. Therese, and I read the story and the prayer inside. Concluding that this all must be of significance, I began a nine-day novena at that very moment for the salvation of my fiancé and our engagement.

On the third day, my prayer was answered. That was the day my fiancé told me he had finally decided to ask God to help him. I believed him, but I still committed to finishing the prayer.

My fiancé went through terrible withdrawals, but he found an awesome Twelve-Step recovery program that has helped him tremendously. Best of all, he has asked Jesus to walk with him each day to keep the compulsion to drink away. It is a true miracle.

I know, with my whole being, that St. Therese wanted me to ask her intercession. The peace and hope I felt when I prayed that first prayer is still tangible. I am thankful to God for creating saints like this, and I thank St. Therese for sharing her love of God and placing that love in my heart. I had an opportunity to thank her in person when her relics visited a nearby church.

Still, the miracles continue. We have had eight nights of frost here. Yesterday, nonetheless, I noticed a miniature rose bush outside that is producing a tiny rosebud despite the fact that there are only three leaves on the entire plant. I have brought the tiny bud inside and will press it in my Bible. I know that my fiancé and I have experienced a special grace from God, an unwarranted and unmerited gift, but, after all, isn't that what grace is?

—*Maura, Nova Scotia, Canada*

Chapter 4

LOVE

Beloved, let us love one another,
for love is from God.

—John 3:11

My Heart's Desire

Ever since I was a little girl growing up in the Philippines, I have loved Jesus. I remember as a child wanting to be with Him always, so much so I would go to church morning and afternoon just to be with Him in the Blessed Sacrament. When I was ten years old, the sister of my best friend introduced me to St. Therese of the Child Jesus. She told me that St. Therese loved Jesus very much and showed it in her little ways, just the way I did, so she thought perhaps I would like to get to know this special saint.

I fell in love with St. Therese right away, and felt an immediate connection. I learned that she often answered prayers with the sign of flowers, so when I asked for her intercession, I would also ask her to send me flowers. One time I was kneeling in front of a life-size statue of the Saint at church, when suddenly three fresh rose petals fell upon me. I looked up to see where they had come from, but there were no fresh roses, just painted flowers around the cross St. Therese was holding. I was truly amazed by this little miracle. I have kept those rose petals for fifty years and they still are bright red and give off a rose scent.

After I had met the Little Flower and witnessed her marvelous intercessory power, I thought that I might also become a Carmelite nun, just like St. Therese. Therefore, I would politely turn down all of my suitors. There was one young man, however, who was different. He was a childhood friend of mine named Rudy. Our families were really close, and Rudy and I grew up together, almost like cousins or brother and sister — or so I thought. Rudy's niece and I were best of friends and spent all of our time together.

Whenever there was a family function, Rudy always came to pick me up.

When the opportunity to join the United States Navy came along, Rudy asked me for my advice. I told him honestly that I thought he would have a better future as a U.S. Navy man. So Rudy moved to America.

While he was there, Rudy's niece asked her uncle for the names of some navy personnel with whom she and her friends could be pen pals. Rudy gave his niece some names, but told her he wanted me to be *his* pen pal. And so we corresponded through the mail. After many letters, Rudy revealed his true feelings for me and offered a proposal of marriage. I was so surprised and confused I stopped writing. When Rudy's father became sick, Rudy returned home to visit him. This time he proposed to me in person, and would not take no for an answer. I told Rudy we needed to pray about this.

Together, we turned to St. Therese and made a novena. We even walked on our knees from the entrance of St. Sebastian Church in Manila all the way to the altar, asking Jesus and St. Therese to help us and let us know if we were meant for each other. I asked for the sign of a yellow rose. During the time of my novena, an aunt invited us over for her son's birthday. As soon as we reached their home, my aunt picked the yellow rose from the birthday cake and gave it to me. I told her about my novena, and my aunt said that Rudy and I were truly meant for one another.

Rudy told me he had also received a positive answer from St. Therese. I was still in denial, however, for my heart's desire was still to be Jesus' bride as a Carmelite nun. In the meantime, Rudy returned to the United States and our communication resumed through letters.

After a year, I was still not absolutely certain about marriage, but I went to America as an immigrant. I stayed in Chicago with Rudy's nieces, where Rudy would come and visit us. On one of his visits, I noticed he was wearing a gold dinner ring with his initials on it. His niece thought Rudy might give me the band as an engagement ring, so she made me try it on. It fit, but I returned the ring to him. On that same visit, Rudy told us it would be several months before we would see him again, as he had received orders that he was getting underway.

After we took Rudy to the airport for his return to the navy base in Norfolk, Virginia, I once again asked St. Therese for a favor. I prayed that if Rudy and I were *truly* meant for one another, he would come back to me within my nine-day novena and present me with that gold dinner ring. I knew this would be near impossible since Rudy's mission was supposed to take several months. However, I also knew that with God, all things are possible. I just wanted to be absolutely certain as my heart still felt a longing to be with Jesus.

On the fourth day of my novena, we heard the doorbell ring at four o'clock in the morning. We looked through the peephole and saw Rudy standing on the doorstep! As soon as we opened the door, he took my hand and put that gold dinner ring on my finger. It turned out his mission had been cancelled and he had three days' leave. He immediately took the first flight back to Chicago. I cried so hard, fully believing it was truly God's plan for Rudy and me to be together. In twelve months' time, Rudy finished his service with the navy and we were married a year later. We have been happily married for thirty-four years with two beautiful children and one wonderful grandson, for whom I am very thankful to God.

Because God knows the longings of our hearts, He did not forget about my childhood desires. Twelve years ago, I made my profession as a Third Order Carmelite and took the name of St. Therese, the Little Flower of Jesus. In this way, I can still live out my cherished vocation as wife and mother, yet I can also serve God as a lay Carmelite, which I came to realize was my true calling.

Just recently, I asked St. Therese for another favor. Rudy and I were asked to go on a pilgrimage to Portugal, Spain, and France, including Lisieux. Ever since I came to know St. Therese, I have wanted to visit her hometown. I prayed and asked the Little Flower to send me white roses if we were to go. On the third day of my novena, three beautiful white roses bloomed in my garden *even though it was December!* We sent in our deposit.

The following February, I was laid off from work. It made finances tight. In April, we were supposed to mail in our final payment for the pilgrimage. Rudy and I went to Mass and I asked St. Therese for another sign, any sign, if we were supposed to go on this trip. Immediately after Mass, a gentleman friend approached me and presented me with a beautiful locket of St. Therese. He said simply, "St. Therese wants you to have this."

We took that as our sign. We mailed in our final payment and trusted God would provide for all our needs. We had a blessed and wonderful pilgrimage. At the basilica in Lisieux, I felt myself being led to a corner where I read the words, "I am your sister and your friend and I will always be watching over you." Then, she blessed us with another miracle. While visiting the Carmelite convent, we had our picture taken in front of the statue of St. Therese. When we had the picture developed, we noticed a heavenly light that seemed to pierce

My husband and I are greeted in a special way on a visit to Lisieux

through her heart and the cross she was carrying and shine down on Rudy and me. I thank Jesus for giving me St. Therese as my sister and my friend and helping me discover my heart's desire.

— *Ulay, Texas*

A Match Made in Heaven

It was around January of 1983 that I prayed a deep and honest novena to St. Therese. I was twenty-seven years old at the time and quite single. As a man of quiet and shy demeanor, I found it difficult to meet and socialize with young ladies. I was lonely and felt the desire to share my life with someone. I turned to St. Therese to ask for help in meeting a young lady who could complete my life and lead me down the path that God had planned for me.

About four months later, a woman named Lea was hired in my office. I was attracted to her immediately and even more so when I found out through talking with her that she was Catholic. Lea and I got along well in the office and, after a few months, we started to date. Once we got to know each other better and found out all of our commonality, our relationship turned serious quickly. Remembering my novena, I turned to St. Therese to give me a sign that Lea was the one that was chosen by God for me.

Within days of making this request of St. Therese, I was with Lea, and she suddenly took the flowered clip out of her hair and handed it to me. I was floored. There was no reason for Lea to give me a hair clip. I could hardly believe what she had done. I shared with her the significance of this action. A few days later, feeling a bit doubtful because it was just a fake floral item and not a real flower, I again prayed to St. Therese. I told her that although I was sure that this was the sign that I had requested, I would like to have a "real" flower as a sign. I did not tell Lea of this prayer.

A couple of days later, Lea met me at the office after work and, as I went to greet her, she handed me a single red rose. Lea and I have been married for almost nineteen years and have four wonderful children. To us, we are a match made in heaven.   — *Bill, California*

Handpicked by God

I have had a devotion to the Little Flower since I was very small. When I grew to be a teenager, despite the turbulent years of adolescence, I thought that I had a vocation — I wanted to be a Carmelite nun.

While in college at the Catholic University of Puerto Rico, I met a wonderful man named Osvaldo whose sister happened to be a nun. We became good friends and talked often about our interest in the religious life. Osvaldo was in his fourth year of premedicine and I was in my third. In time, we started dating, and I discovered I had feelings for him. In my heart, however, I still was serious about becoming a nun.

One night, during an Honor Society biology convention, Osvaldo confided to me that he liked me. I did not know how to respond. To sort out my confused feelings, I had been praying to my spiritual friend, St. Therese, to let me know with the sign of roses what the will of God was, and I had not yet received an answer.

The next day was Sunday, and Osvaldo drove me and some of our college friends to Sunday Mass at my parish. After Mass, we returned to the science convention. When it was over, we piled back into Osvaldo's car, but he insisted that I sit on the seat next to him. We began driving home. All of the sudden, Osvaldo stopped the car and jumped out. To my surprise, he jumped over a wire fence. I had no idea what he was doing. None of us did. As I watched, I saw him approach a rose bush and cut off three roses. He brought them to me — one was white, one dark pink, and the other yellow. When he handed me the little bouquet, I immediately thought of St. Therese and my prayer to her. Our friends thought this was very romantic, but none of them — not even Osvaldo — knew of the significance of this gesture. To me, however, it was confirmation that God handpicked this man.

Today, Osvaldo and I have been happily married for forty-one years. That was only the first of many miracles with which St. Therese would bless our lives.

— *Maribelle, Florida*

I Believe in Love

I was raised Catholic but was never into my faith until I went to college. My first two years were spent at Auburn University in Alabama, where I first began to experience the love of God and His mercy through the help of a priest named Father Dean.

Father Dean was a very prayerful and knowledgeable priest who loved the Church, her teachings, and her saints. He took me under his wing and began to teach me about God, the Church, truth, and prayer. After about eight months of intense life-changing events, I decided I would like to spend a week in prayerful solitude. I made plans to leave Auburn and go to College Station, Texas, to experience a silent retreat under the guidance of another priest whose name, oddly enough, was also Father Dean.

The day before I left for Texas, Father Dean told me he had a book that he wanted me to read during my retreat. The book was called *I Believe in Love: A Personal Retreat Based on the Teaching of St. Therese of Lisieux*, by Jean C. J. d'Elbee. Though I knew nothing about this saint, I accepted the book and promised to read it.

Three days later, I found myself in a cabin on a farm in Texas, away from friends, family, and familiarity. I began my retreat with a simple prayer, "Lord, I want to grow in You, be with me." Little did I realize this retreat would change my life forever.

One hot Texas afternoon, I cracked open the old book given to me by Father Dean and immediately I knew God was at work. For the next five days, I pored over its pages and was amazed at what I found. I read of humble confidence in

Jesus, of a "little way" of life that could change the world. I learned of the love God has for me, just like a father for a child. I began to realize that I was Jesus' precious one, just like Therese.

After five days of the Holy Spirit filling me with His wisdom and love through the intercession of St. Therese, needless to say, a relationship began for me with this great saint.

I returned to college in Auburn a different man. People noticed the change immediately. I told them of my time alone with Jesus and Therese. My enthusiasm about the book I'd read inspired many of my friends to find a copy. After a few months more at Auburn, almost floating with the love of God inside me, I felt called to lead a life of Church work. I left Auburn University to attend Franciscan University in Steubenville, Ohio. There, I would soon discover once again that my sister St. Therese would have another dramatic impact on my life.

After about six months at school, I met a girl named Heather. She sang at Mass and had a spirituality and depth to her that literally made my mouth drop. She was amazing, with a voice like an angel, and I could hear the voice of God beautifully through her. We became good friends and talked all the time. I told her of my desire to have children and experience marriage and family as God intended it. Heather told me of her dreams and hopes as well.

Not too long after we met, I began to feel love for this woman but, in my mind, she was too spiritually advanced, too holy. She was more like a mentor than a girlfriend. However, like Therese, I loved to get my way.

After we had known each other for several more months, Heather and I began to date. I had dated lots of girls and knew that Heather was someone exceptional. Women like her did not come around often. I began to think of marriage and children; my heart began to spin and dance.

After eight months of dating, I knew this was the woman I wanted to marry. Heather and I had talked about marriage, and we knew that dating was about finding your spouse, not about wasting time and money (which I was guilty of before I met Heather). I knew she was the one, but how could I ask this amazing woman to marry me in a way that was telling of my love for her? Once again, Therese came to my rescue. I decided I would pray a novena to St. Therese and ask Heather to marry me on her feast day, October 1.

The plans were set, and the final day of the novena arrived. I went through the day, my heart pounding and mind racing, but my soul was at peace. I picked Heather up from her house and told her I had to stop by my office at the university to run a quick errand. The plan was running perfectly. It just so happened (not by coincidence, of course) that we were standing right next to the entrance of a tiny chapel that was in my office building. I asked Heather if she would like to go in and pray for a minute.

This was the moment of truth. In the presence of the Lord, we sat down. My heart beat as if I had just run a marathon (later Heather told me she could actually hear my heart beating). After about a minute of feeling the blood sprint through my body, I got down on one knee and said, "Heather, I love you. You are the most important person in my life, and I want to run the race with you." (This was an important Scripture passage in our relationship: Hebrews 12:1)

I bent over and took out a basin of water that was set in place prior to our arrival. I took off Heather's shoes and socks and began to wash her feet. I said, "Husbands love your wives as Christ loved the Church and gave Himself up for her, that He might sanctify her, having cleansed her by the washing of water with the word" (Ephesians 5:25). I then reached underneath Heather's seat and took out a little Bible. It was a Bible that she was wanting for some time, but could not find. I happened to spot it that day in a Christian bookstore. (Later, when Heather and I went to the store to thank them for stocking a Catholic Bible, we were surprised to hear they had never ordered such a book.) Engraved on the front of the Bible was Heather's name with my last name.

I then told Heather to look underneath the tabernacle. I had placed a dozen long-stem red roses there. I told Heather they were from St. Therese and let her know I had prayed a novena that the Little Flower would be an intercessor in our engagement and in our marriage. Finally, I turned to Heather and asked her to marry me. She said, "Yes!" and we hugged and cried.

Weeks later, Heather and I were reflecting on our engagement, and Heather shared something amazing. She told me that the most powerful part of our engagement was the novena and roses from St. Therese. She relayed that long before we met, she would ask St. Therese daily to protect her future spouse — to let him know he is loved and to prepare him for our lives together.

When Heather told me this, my curiosity was piqued. I asked her when specifically this prayer was taking place. Sure enough, Heather was intensely praying for her future spouse, through St. Therese, at the *exact time* I was experiencing my conversion on retreat in Texas!

Eight months later, Heather and I were married. Our excitement to start a family, however, was diminished when

we faced unexpected fertility problems. After several unsuccessful attempts to conceive, we had almost lost hope. But
one day Heather was at daily Mass offering her constant intention that we could have a child. Suddenly, a voice spoke
softly in her ear, "Maria Therese." Heather was puzzled at
this random thought. She concluded it meant we should
ask St. Therese and Our Lady for their intercession to have
children. We began to pray, and on the feast of the Annunciation, Heather and I found out we were pregnant. Eight
months later, Heather gave birth to a little girl named Maria
Therese. She is healthy and beautiful and an absolute gift
from God.   —Jake, Colorado

Love Enshrined

My grandmother introduced me to St. Therese when
I was twenty-seven years old, and she and my grandfather would visit me in my apartment. One day the
topic of the patron saint of my middle name, Theresa, came
up. I confessed I didn't know much about St. Therese of
Lisieux except that I had heard she answered prayers with
a "shower of roses." The next time they came to visit, my
grandmother brought me some little books of saints with a
paragraph or two about St. Therese along with a small statue
of my patron and a novena prayer card. After reading them,
I kept them in a drawer by my bedside.

A couple of years later, I started dating Ken, whom I would
later marry. The first months of dating went so well that
I decided to say a novena to determine whether Ken was
the "one." I said my novena in November and kept vigilant

watch for a shower of roses, in whatever form St. Therese wished to send them.

A few weeks later, while I was still patiently watching and waiting, Ken invited me to go to Mass at his parish, the Shrine Church in Royal Oak. During the Eucharistic Prayer, I suddenly realized my novena had been answered. The priest proclaimed the name of the church's patron saint: St. Therese, the Little Flower. I nearly fell off the kneeler as it dawned on me that St. Therese hadn't sent me a shower of roses — she sent me to her church, instead! Until that day, I hadn't realized that the church's full name was "Shrine of the Little Flower" (now the National Shrine), and the first church dedicated to St. Therese after she was canonized.

A few months after that, in March, my grandmother passed away. Visitation at the funeral home was on my thir-tieth birthday. I spent the first half of the day teaching, holding back my emotions while I directed rehearsals for an upcoming school concert. During one rehearsal, the sec-retary walked into the gym carrying a dozen roses from Ken for my birthday. At that moment, I was caught up in the emotions and events of the day. Later that night, however, I made the connection: my grandmother was in heaven with St. Therese, and I received roses from both of them through Ken, my future husband. The coincidence was too much, and I was overwhelmed by the goodness of St. Therese. I still get chills thinking about it!

Ken and I were married the next year and continued to attend the Shrine of the Little Flower church. A couple of years into our marriage, we wanted to start a family. I had a miscarriage, and then months passed without us conceiving. My doctor wanted to put me on a mild fertility drug, but I wanted to avoid that. Instead, I said a novena to St. Therese.

*National Shrine of
the Little Flower,
Royal Oak, Michigan
Photo credit: Rita K. Tinetti*

The day before I had planned to take a home pregnancy test, I received a friendly note from my sister-in-law. I knew my prayer was answered when I saw that the front of the card was covered with bouquets of roses. Sure enough, I was pregnant! We decided that if the baby were a girl, her name would be Angela Rose, after the shower of roses we received from St. Therese.

Little "showers," not always in the form of roses, continued to occur. The Shrine was one of the fortunate churches to be selected as a stop on the tour of St. Therese's relics. The scheduled date for the relics to arrive was November 3, and the baby's due date was November 2. Angela Rose was born on October 29, arriving home just as the relics arrived at the church. Her paternal grandparents, on their first visit to see her in the hospital, brought not just flowers, but a rosebush! To this day, we call the plant an Angela Rose, and it blooms regularly. Angela now keeps the little statue of St. Therese that my grandparents bought for me in her room. Sometimes it is on her nightstand, and sometimes she sleeps with it.

I have been actively involved with my music fraternity, Sigma Alpha Iota, for fourteen years. St. Therese is sending showers of roses through that, too, as the flower of the fraternity is the red rose, and just last year I received an award: the Rose of Honor.

We now have two children, Angela Rose and Jenna Marie, and both have been baptized at the Shrine. We continue to attend Mass there, and have enrolled Angela in its school. We intend to stay and raise our daughters in this strong faith community, and one day they will come to understand the impact St. Therese has had on our lives. My faith in St. Therese grows as I marvel at the little miracles she continues to do for us. — *Marie Theresa, Michigan*

When Miracles Come to Bloom

A few years ago, I started praying for something harder than I have ever prayed for anything in my entire life. It is incredibly dear to my heart and involves reuniting with a woman who is most special to me. I was praying constantly from the deepest part of my heart, as sincerely as possible, asking God for help. In His infinite wisdom and grace, God sent me someone remarkable to assist me, by the name of St. Therese of Lisieux.

My introduction to the Little Flower came while I was attending daily Mass in the town where I practiced medicine. After Mass, a woman I didn't know walked up to me and told me "she liked me for some reason" and handed me a book of prayers to St. Therese of Lisieux. As a convert to the Catholic faith, I had never heard of this saint, so I put the book away for several weeks. One Sunday, however, I felt almost compelled to read the little book after Mass.

While it did not tell me anything about St. Therese's life, the book did explain how devotion to this saint started, how the priest who began the first novena requested that Therese would pray along with him to God for "one great favor," something really important. The priest asked that if God were going to grant what he was asking, Therese would send him a rose to let him know. The story went on to say how he received his rose in an unusual manner and his prayers were answered. This happened twice.

I was fascinated by this story. Imagine, a saint who uses physical, tangible things to guide a person as to what God's will is in a situation. I looked up to heaven and said, "St. Therese, I don't know who you are, but I like your style. I need your help. I am going to pray every day for one thing, and one thing only. If God is going to let it happen, then you must let me know. The rose thing is good. I don't understand it all, but whatever you do, it has to be obvious, because I really need to know what to do here. Thank you." Then I told her what my "great favor" was and began my diligent prayers.

Almost immediately, things began to happen. I found out that the feast day of St. Therese, the day the Church cele-brates her earthly life, is October 1. Ironically, October 1 is also the birthday of the woman with whom I wished to be reunited. I was stunned.

Then, I received a rose. I was making a holy hour in front of the Blessed Sacrament. Exhausted from work, I dozed off only to be awakened when a woman hurried in, dropped a cellophane-wrapped rose at the base of the statue of Mary, and left just as quickly. The next day, I received a phone message out of the blue from the woman who was the focus of my prayers.

Another time, I had flooding in my garage that drenched a cardboard box full of medical books, ruining them all. As I was unpacking the mess, I discovered to my great surprise a prayer book to St. Therese that I had no recollection of owning. It was the only religious article in the box — and the only book to remain bone dry.

Late that night, I got a call from the woman of my affections. She called to tell me she had been in a serious car crash but miraculously was not injured at all. I shared with her what had been happening. She wasn't sure what to make of it. I sent her the prayer book and continued my prayers all the more fervently.

Time passed, and I did not hear from her. I was beginning to feel very disillusioned. One spring afternoon, I was doing several hours of yard work. My mower maneuvered around numerous bushes that grew on my property, plants that had never bloomed in the six years I had owned the house. I hated these bushes. They were ugly and they scratched me whenever I mowed. Looking closer, I noticed they were all gray, dried up, and lifeless. "Good," I thought to myself. "They're dead. Now I won't feel so guilty about chopping them down!" By the time I got my clippers out, however, darkness fell. It would have to wait until the following day.

*Property explodes with rose blossoms
on the anniversary of St. Therese's canonization*

The next day was Sunday, May 17. I was carrying my recyclable bin to the end of my driveway before going to Mass. When I turned around and faced my house I quite literally almost fainted at what I saw. *Every plant capable of bearing roses on my property had all bloomed simultaneously that morning.* On dead limbs without any sign of life whatsoever, grew hundreds, maybe thousands of roses! I stood there, shocked, not believing my eyes. Then, I ran into my house, grabbed a disposable camera, and began snapping pictures frantically. I was afraid the flowers would disappear all of a sudden. After all, they had appeared so suddenly — just twelve hours earlier, there wasn't even a bud. As I took the pictures, I realized other plants around the house had also bloomed. There were even some green leafy bushes that I had tied to shape into round balls since they had never done anything but grow green leaves. They, too, were covered with roses — and I had no idea they were even rose bushes! Convinced this was a miracle, I raced some blooms over to the Grotto Shrine at the seminary of Mount Saint Mary's

College. I found the monsignor, a retired president of the seminary, a noted theologian, and longtime chaplain of the Shrine and its gardens. Studying my pictures, he confirmed that in fifty years of tending roses at the Grotto, he never saw anything like this. To him, it was a miracle.

A fellow parishioner who was a retired FBI special agent contacted professors of botany, horticulture experts, and owners of commercial rose nurseries to examine the phenomenon. They all said the same thing — there was no scientific explanation for the timing or profuseness of rose blooms on those plants.

A second priest from Michigan, with expertise in investigating and evaluating religious phenomena, heard of my story and arranged to meet with me and examine my pictures. He also found the event quite extraordinary. Once he became involved in the investigation, amazing things began happening to him, including his receipt of a first-class relic of St. Therese from someone unaware of the story. Astonishingly, the priest gave this precious relic to me, concluding that it was meant to be mine.

Even more amazing, when I told him the date the roses bloomed, the priest informed me that May 17 was the date St. Therese of Lisieux was canonized — the date she was officially declared a saint! There is no doubt in my mind whatsoever that this miracle was connected with the Little Flower.

Many, many other marvelous things have happened to me, too numerous to mention here, and still, the story — like a flower — continues to unfold. I only know in my heart that no matter what the outcome, one woman who will always be in my life is St. Therese of Lisieux.

—Jim, North Carolina

Chapter 5

‘HEALING

I will restore you to health
and I will heal you of your wounds,
declares the Lord.

—Jeremiah 30:17

Sam's Cure

My husband, Sam, suffered a stroke at work on April 19, 1999. He was taken to Mother Cabrini Hospital in New York and then transferred to Mount Sinai Hospital and admitted in their neurological intensive care unit. That night, Sam was unable to speak coherently. He was scheduled for an angiogram the following day to identify the cause of the stroke. Immediately, friends and family joined our prayers.

The angiogram revealed that Sam was born with an arterial venous malformation (AVM) and that one of the walls of one of the arteries had bled, causing Sam to have a stroke. Unfortunately, the AVM was in an inoperable part of the brain. Surgery could kill Sam, the doctors explained, or leave him a human vegetable. His chance of survival was only 30 percent and, even if he did survive, he would not be the same person as before. Since there was a chance that the AVM could bleed again, we were told to make sure Sam was never far from a neurological ICU.

Life changed dramatically for Sam. He could not travel. He could not work. He could not leave the house without a cell phone to use in case of an emergency. He needed to be hooked up to a Metro Alert machine. Needless to say, Sam was miserable in his new state.

Meanwhile, I continued to pray, as did my family and friends. I have a devotion to the Blessed Mother and fervently offered prayers and fasts for her intercession. One Sunday, after Mass, I picked up the local Catholic newspaper, which featured a picture on the back page of a saint I knew only vaguely — St. Therese of Lisieux. It said that her relics would be visiting St. Patrick's Cathedral. When we arrived home, I cut the back page out and taped it to the inside of our front door where I could see it every day. I told Sam we had to go to visit the relics of this saint, as I had a feeling she could help him.

When the weekend arrived that the relics were in town, one of my friends called and said the lines were very long. I knew that Sam could not stand in line for three hours, so we went at 4:00 a.m. on October 19, coincidentally Sam's birthday. The wait in line took approximately a half hour. Sam and I approached the relics of St. Therese and both laid our hands on the protective shield guarding the relics. Afterward, we sat down and stayed until the departure ceremony at 6:00 a.m. was over. When they processed the relics out of the cathedral, I felt a sadness and heard a little voice inside me say, "Please don't go. . . . "

Later that month, on October 28, Sam and I went to Columbia Presbyterian Hospital to meet with a skilled brain surgeon. The surgeon told us that Sam was an excellent candidate for Gamma Knife surgery. Normally, there was a waiting list of two to three years for such an operation but because of the seriousness of Sam's condition, he was moved to the top of the list. Surgery was scheduled for December 6, 1999.

We arrived at the hospital at 5:30 a.m. Gamma Knife surgery is a very precise technology that has absolutely no room for error. The Knife's 201 radiation rays had to be a direct hit, or there could be dire consequences for the patient. Therefore, to ensure the immobilization of Sam's head during the operation, he was first fitted with a metal band that was literally screwed into his skull. This band would support a wooden scaffolding that would allow him to be fitted with a special plastic helmet.

Before surgery, Sam was sent for a special imaging scan to pinpoint the AVM. We were told ahead of time that Sam might need an angiogram, but the doctors promised they would try to avoid one if possible since it could kill or impair a patient if a stroke occurred. Unfortunately for Sam, it was determined that he would need one. They made Sam sign the necessary papers stating he understood the serious consequences of the angiogram. Then I was told to leave and return in an hour and a half.

About ninety minutes later, I anxiously returned. Finally, the surgeon appeared announcing he had good news. I thought the good news was that Sam was not dead.

The doctor said, "Sam has been totally cured. In medicine, we call this spontaneous healing. It is rare. However, there are records of it. We could not find any trace of the AVM on the scan. That's why we ordered the angiogram. It proved to us that the AVM has completely disappeared. It's as if Sam had the Gamma Knife surgery over two years ago and we were doing a follow-up exam today. There's simply nothing there."

Immediately, I knew what had happened. I told the doctor excitedly about praying at the relics of St. Therese. "Well," the doctor replied. "God has answered your prayers. You can take your husband home tonight."

I was stunned. I kept wondering if I were hallucinating. Was I out of my mind? Then it sunk in. It was true — I was not dreaming. Sam was cured!

That evening and the following days were spent marveling at the blessing God had given Sam. I thought about how everyone had prayed. I thought about St. Therese, and I was thoroughly convinced that she and the Blessed Mother had interceded on Sam's birthday to seek from God this priceless gift of healing.   —*Frances, New York*

He Looks Like a Rose

I have a friend named Mary Jane who is married and the mother of five children. Several years ago, Mary Jane's twenty-five-year-old son, Bob, had a dreadful automobile accident. Driving alone on a rain-slicked road, he came upon a curve, lost control, and hit a telephone pole. He was not wearing a seat belt and landed on the floorboard of the passenger side of the car.

The irony is that had Bob been wearing a seat belt, he probably would have been killed instantly. The engine had backed right up into the driver's side and most certainly would have crushed him to death.

Mary Jane and her husband were called by the doctor and told that Bob's condition was critical and that emergency surgery was necessary to remove the spleen. He hastened to add his fear that Bob might not survive surgery; however, there was no choice. He told them there was brain damage; how extensive they did not know at this point. In addition, there were internal injuries, and this made the prospect of recovery grim.

Bob's condition went from bad to worse. He had to be hooked up to a life support system. The anguish of his physical suffering was surpassed only by the fear of his dying. Looking down at the almost lifeless body of her son, Mary Jane thought of the Blessed Mother and how she must have felt at the foot of the cross. Invoking Mary's intercession, she pleaded for the life of her son.

For the next three days and nights, there was virtually no change in Bob's condition, and the doctors held out little hope. They said he could remain in a coma indefinitely. On the other hand, he could die suddenly! Mary Jane sat by her son's bedside in intensive care. Staring at the wall, she whispered to God: "There is nothing I can do — Bob is yours." Her mind was flooded with a kaleidoscope of images of Bob from the time he was born to the present moment.

Realizing what a fragile and precious gift life is, Mary Jane took her son's hand into her own and began to pray a novena to St. Therese of Lisieux. She had just finished the prayers for the first day when an intern walked into the room and announced they were going to attempt to take Bob off the breathing machine to see if he could breathe on his own. Mary Jane felt a tightening in her chest.

She could not bear to stand by and watch Bob struggling for his very breath. And, if he regained consciousness, she did not want him to see her in such a state. "He may die," she thought. "Dear God, please help me to accept Your will."

After what seemed an eternity, the intern poked his head in the doorway of the visitor's lounge where Mary Jane anxiously waited. Clutching the arms of her chair like a vise, Mary Jane braced herself for the worst. The intern smiled and told her Bob was able to breathe on his own.

Mary Jane, in disbelief, followed the intern back to her son's room. Bob was in a deep coma, but breathing without effort. His face, no longer obstructed by tubes, was a beautiful sight to behold. The intern observed Bob carefully for a minute or two and then gazing over at Mary Jane, said, "Doesn't he look like a rose?"

Astonished, Mary Jane raised her head and stared at the doctor in amazement. "What a choice of words," she said without explanation. The novena she had barely begun was still fresh in her mind. Already St. Therese had given her a sign! The devastating fear and anxiety of the past four days disappeared in that instant.

Mary Jane's face was aglow as she walked out into the hall. A nurse approached her and said, "You look like your son has been given back to you." "It's true," Mary Jane beamed. "I really feel like he has been born again!" The fact that Bob was still in a coma had not diminished Mary Jane's feelings one bit. She was too busy marveling at the resourcefulness of God. "Imagine the doctor comparing Bob to a rose," she smiled to herself.

The following day when she saw the intern, she could not resist the temptation to ask if he had ever described any of his patients as looking like a flower.

"No," the intern confessed. "I really have no idea why I said that. You were so visibly touched that later I thought perhaps 'Rose' might be the name of someone near and dear to Bob." To that Mary Jane simply acknowledged it did indeed mean something very special to her.

Bob did not miraculously rise from his bed. He remained in and out of a comatose state for some time. The doctors continued to report messages of gloom and doom. They told Mary Jane that Bob had permanent brain damage and, even if he came out of the coma, it was unlikely that he would ever function normally.

Despite pessimistic pronouncements, Bob improved little by little. After six months, he was placed in a rehabilitation center and, when he was able, he moved back home with his family.

Today Bob's speech and motor development are normal. He is back on his feet physically, emotionally, and financially. The doctors have no explanation. All the signs had pointed to permanent disability — all except one: the rose plucked from God's heavenly garden and placed on the lips of the intern that day.   — *Marion, Maryland*

My Mother's Healing

I was born and raised in London, Ontario, Canada, the eldest of seven children. When I was nine years old, my mother was expecting a child. Midterm in her pregnancy she developed yellow atrophy of the liver and her liver stopped functioning. The doctor told my father to make arrangements as to who would raise his children as my mother would die certainly within a short period of time. It was a foregone conclusion that the child within my mother's womb would also die as it was too young to survive.

My father was devastated. The four children were parceled out to live with relatives while my father and his brothers desperately donated blood to try to keep my mother and the baby alive.

When my grandparents heard the terrible news that their daughter was dying and so was their grandchild, they immediately contacted the sisters at a Carmelite Monastery near their home in Kitchener, Ontario. The nuns had a miraculous portrait of the Little Flower that they would lend to others who had been ill. My grandmother called the Carmelites from the hospital and the painting was put on the next train to London.

Two hours later as the train arrived at the station, a medical team was monitoring my mother's vital signs at the hospital. Witnesses said that at the precise moment that the train arrived, the hospital room filled completely with the scent of roses. My grandmother said, "She is here. The Little Flower has arrived."

The nurses who were monitoring my mother's vital signs reported that she had somehow "reversed" and her pulse and heartbeat were unexpectedly stronger. As the scent of roses became stronger and stronger, so did my mother. The doctors, disbelieving, came in to check. Smelling the roses, the chief of staff asked a nurse to remove the flowers from the room, as my mother needed all of the oxygen she could get. She replied that there were no flowers, and they had no idea of the origin of the scent of the roses. Gradually, through the night, my mother's vital signs returned to normal.

By dawn, my mother was conscious and seemed on the road to recovery. Later in the morning, the doctors told the family that my mother would probably survive but they could not tell how or why. In 1952, my mother was the second person in history (as documented by the Medical Association in Britain) to have survived this disease. The doctors also said that because my mother had lost so much oxygen, the baby would probably be miscarried.

My mother was kept at the hospital in anticipation of the miscarriage until it became obvious that the child was still alive. She was warned that through the next several weeks she could expect a miscarriage; therefore she was ordered to have complete bed rest on her return home. The child continued to grow. The doctors became increasingly worried that the baby would probably not survive birth and, if it did, it would no doubt be mentally retarded or terribly handicapped with the trauma of the collapse of the liver and damage to my mother's blood supply.

However, on January 5, 1953, my baby sister was born healthy and strong. The doctor who delivered her broke down in tears saying, "It's a miracle. She is as big as a Christmas turkey!" The child, referred to as the "miracle baby" by the hospital staff for years, grew up strong and bright — so strong, in fact, she was a Canadian tennis champion and is now head of the Department of Physical Education at McMaster University in Hamilton, Ontario. My sister is a wonderful professional woman who quietly keeps the secret why she is named Therese.　　　— *Father John, Switzerland*

Ecumenical Healer

In 1975, our third daughter, Roseann, was born on February 2. She appeared to be a healthy baby and was baptized when she was about three weeks old. Shortly after, Roseann developed a cold that went into her chest. After we took her to the doctor for three consecutive days because she could no longer nurse without great discomfort, she was hospitalized in an oxygen tent. I could not believe she was so ill, since I was breastfeeding her and believed that breast milk should protect babies from illness. As it turned out, there was some sort of flu that was putting so many small children in the hospital that they were running out of beds.

The night before Roseann was hospitalized, I had picked up my little blue prayer book and said many prayers for my baby's recovery, including one to St. Therese. The following afternoon, after getting home from the hospital, I found a beautiful bouquet of yellow roses on our kitchen table. Our oldest daughter had ridden home from school with a neighbor and, when the neighbor was driving past a flower shop, she thought it would be nice to give us flowers on the birth of our newest daughter. This was a woman that I had met once or twice and didn't really know very well.

That night, I returned to my prayer book and began to pray. When I got to the prayer to St. Therese, I read about the promise of roses to those whose favors would be granted. The next morning, I told my husband, Glenn, about the connection between St. Therese and roses. Sure enough, after nine days in the hospital, Roseann came home healthy.

Glenn, a public school psychologist, was impressed by the results of my prayer, and told some of his colleagues about St. Therese, the roses, and Roseann. Nearly all the people he told were very skeptical, thinking it to be a superstitious story. However, one man named Murray, who was Jewish, remembered my husband's story when he developed sciatica later in the spring. Despite the care of a physician and medication, Murray's pain was not relieved. When it got to the point where he could barely walk, Murray asked my husband to pray to St. Therese for a cure. Of course, my husband agreed.

On Monday, after Easter break, Glenn was getting out of his car when he spotted Murray running toward him. Murray could hardly wait to tell him about "his" rose. The previous week, Murray had taught his Wednesday night Spanish class for adults. During the break that night, a woman came up and handed him a single rose. He asked why she had brought him a flower. She said that it was the only rose in her garden, and she thought it would be nice to give it to him. After the break, Murray told his class about St. Therese and roses, and there were quite a few tears among his students. Needless to say, Murray was cured of his sciatica.

Then the wife of one of Glenn's colleagues was diagnosed with cancer. Her husband had listened to Glenn's story about St. Therese and the roses and, although neither he nor his wife were Catholic, he asked my husband to pray for her. The day before the lady was scheduled to go in for surgery, two of her children came home and presented her with some roses. It turns out they had gone by someone's yard on the way home from school and picked the flowers, something they were not supposed to do. This time, however, their mother accepted them gratefully. When she went into the hospital the next day for her surgery, the doctors found no cancer where it had been detected the previous week.

I still pray to St. Therese, even if it's only asking her to pray for us. She will always be considered one of my favorite saints. I've learned through my experiences with her that it isn't critical which faith you belong to when it comes to the intercession of St. Therese. All that's important is that you have faith in her heavenly help through God.

—*Ann, California*

A New Woman

I have been a fervent prayer to Ste-Thérèse for about five years, and she has bestowed so many roses my way. Two years ago, my prayers were directed toward this saint on behalf of my daughter, Angèle. She had been using illegal drugs for many years, which led her to quit the university. Then she left for Montreal, where drugs could be found in more abundance. Angèle couldn't keep a job, she had an abortion, and she suffered from one depression after another.

I prayed to Ste-Thérèse to bring my daughter back home and to put good people on her road. Once I got Ste-Thérèse involved, the whole situation changed. My daughter returned home to our small community. She got herself a job and began to cut down on drugs. I kept praying.

Since then, Angèle has been to a rehabilitation center and is now seeing a drug counselor. I'm happy to announce she has been drug-free for several months. My daughter is seeing a psychologist regularly and has started a new job that she really likes. She is even talking of going back to the university. At twenty-four, she is a new woman. So many thanks to Ste-Thérèse!   — *Madeleine, Ontario, Canada*

Survivors

I visited the relics of St. Therese with my best friend several years ago when she was battling breast cancer. It is the only time I have ever visited the relics of a saint, and it touched me very deeply. I prayed to St. Therese for the recovery of my friend for many months afterward.

Two years later, I also was diagnosed with breast cancer. Fortunately I had a prayer card and a pin from my visit to St. Therese's relics. I set them by my bedside as I faced my own battle.

I'm happy to say, both my best friend and I are breast cancer survivors, she four years, I, one and a half years.

St. Therese's prayer card and pin still sit on my bedside table and I pray to her daily.

Interestingly, at Easter time, my sister gave me a most unusual and beautiful gift. Totally unaware of my affinity with St. Therese, but well aware of my love of antiques, she purchased a charm bracelet full of antique crosses and medals. Upon closer inspection, I realized that one of the medals was of my patron saint, St. Anne, and the remaining four were all St. Therese medals. An odd coincidence? It could be. I prefer to believe it's a reminder that the Little Flower is spending her "heaven doing good on earth."

— Cindy, California

Back Injury

I have had a devotion to St. Therese, the Little Flower, since I was a child in grade school at St. Agnes School in Rockville Center, New York. My teacher, a Dominican sister, read the story of St. Therese of Lisieux to our first grade class. It was the early 1950s. Shortly after, my mother did something to injure her back that left her in extreme pain.

My mother was always a very active and energetic person. However, she had faced her fair share of challenges. She was pregnant with me at forty-two years of age, during which time her oldest son, my brother George, was killed in combat in World War II. My father was paralyzed due to a major stroke, and one of my adult brothers who lived at home with us was mentally retarded and an epileptic. She certainly had her hands full! However, she seemed to take this all in stride because of her great faith in God and a determination to do what was right.

What was frightening to me about the incident with her back was that this seemingly small injury had made her un-characteristically take to her bed. It was hard to see her so defeated. I decided right then, in secret, to make a novena to St. Therese to help my mother be well again.

This happened early in the fall, and I soon forgot all about it. My mother remained in pain for what seemed to me a very long time. My brother Tom, who was married and lived near us with his wife and baby girls, asked if my mother and I would come to babysit while he and his wife went out. My mother only reluctantly agreed because of her back pain.

That evening, after returning home, my brother was see-ing us to the door and discovered a rose blooming in his garden in front of the house. It was a beautiful red rose and was very unusual because this was the month of November, just before Thanksgiving, in fact. Tom picked the rose and gave it to me. I didn't make the connection.

The next morning, I awoke to my mother's voice outside, singing at the top of her lungs. This was something she had always done while she was working, but it had ceased during the time of her back pain. Surprised, I ran to see what was happening and discovered my mother outside on our porch sweeping, cleaning, and singing. I asked her if her back was okay now, and she said that it was very strange indeed — she woke up that morning and the pain was completely gone!

It was then that I finally made the connection of my novena to St. Therese and the November rose.

As a result of this incident, which was quite impressive to a young child, I have maintained a very strong devo-tion to St. Therese my entire life. I am now fifty-eight years old and still believe that the Little Flower sent a blessing to my mother and me. The rose is proof enough for me!

— *Barbara, New Jersey*

In Life and in Death

Our intimate friendship with St. Therese started with the carrying of our second infant, Christopher John, destined to live his life entirely within his mother's womb. In short, the specialists told us to abort our darling child; we continued to trust in the Lord and knew that we would have an answer to our little one's health concerns by the feast day of St. Therese, October 1, 1996. The doctors marveled at our faith and, in the Little Flower's way and through an act of mercy from God, sweet Christopher John was born on October 1 and carried away to heaven. During the difficult delivery, I prayed for St. Therese to help me because I knew that our first son had completed his journey on earth. At that moment, I felt an indescribable peace. I felt her presence in a very tangible way and knew that St. Therese was with me. In her honor, our baby's gravestone bears the notation, "Our Heavenly Rose."

In her gentle, reassuring ways, St. Therese continued to help us cope with our loss. In the early days after the funeral, I had been crying on the telephone with my mother. When I got off the phone, my three-year-old daughter, Hanna, opened the sliding patio door without a word. She went outside, picked a rosebud from a nearby bush (although it was November), and handed it to me. My spirits were lifted and once again our eyes raised to heaven.

OUR HEAVENLY ROSE
CHRISTOPHER JOHN ELIOT
OCTOBER 1, 1996

St. Therese helps us in our sorrows and our joys

For months after, I would know to the day how many weeks had passed since we laid our precious one to rest. On the morning of the seventh month, I stood in our garden window praying to St. Therese and Christopher in heaven, and seven rose petals fell, one by one, from a rose I had earlier placed on the window sill in a vase before a statue of Our Lady.

When I was pregnant with my fourth child, Jack Christopher, St. Therese continued to send us roses to let us know this baby would be fine. When I was rushed to the hospital ten weeks before my due date, I clung to this promise of roses. An emergency C-section was scheduled. The specialists in the room were grim because the baby had not moved for several minutes and was not responding to stimuli. They called my husband to come to the hospital immediately, where he was greeted with dire predictions regarding our baby's survival.

They rushed me into the operating room and performed the emergency C-section. When Jack was delivered, I heard this tiny whimper of a cry and heard the doctors urging, "Breathe, Jack, breathe!" I could scarcely breathe myself. With that, they whisked Jack upstairs to NICU. Tears rolled down my cheeks as the tiny little one was taken upstairs to begin his fight for life.

In sum, Jack Christopher proved to be something of a fighter! He was soon weaned from a ventilator and placed under an oxygen hood, his little eyes taped shut and tubes and wires everywhere. We kept a vigil by his incubator and adorned the glass with St. Therese holy cards. Every so often, one of his little neighbors would be rushed over to the local children's hospital. We felt blessed to be able to keep Jack in NICU. Although his eight-week stay there had its medical ups and downs, St. Therese sent us many roses and Jack emerged unscathed by any of the maladies that typically accompany a premature birth.

During Jack's hospital ordeal, we became close to a Benedictine abbot named Leo, and we told him about our experience with St. Therese. Not long after, I was praying a novena to the Little Flower to send me a sign if I was again with child. On the last day of my novena, I received from Abbot Leo a beautiful photograph of our sweet saint in a pamphlet about her relics tour. I was indeed pregnant, and once again, St. Therese was making the journey with us.

I have a cousin who is gifted with special spiritual abilities. Throughout my pregnancy with this fifth child, she wrote me letters saying that I should not worry, the baby is struggling, but Christopher John was with her and helping her. I did not understand these letters at the time, because this pregnancy was proceeding smoothly. I tended to dismiss the letters in a way, thinking my cousin must be confusing this pregnancy with my earlier ones. Whenever I would begin to feel the least bit anxious, I prayed to St. Therese and she always sent me roses.

By this time, my husband and I knew we would name the baby "Grace," for God's love. I had not given my cousin this information. However, in the midst of her sending me the troubling letters, she also sent me a plaque entitled "Everything is Grace," with a picture of St. Therese and the rest of the Little Flower's famous quote.

Based on my past history, my doctor scheduled me for a C-section on June 26, 2000. That morning, my husband and I heard the song "Amazing Grace" on the radio. We took that as a sign that all would be well with the baby, despite the latest letter from my cousin in which she told me I would have angels around me.

While prepping for the C-section, labor started naturally and my OB advised us to let things run their course. He left to check on other patients and our nurse, fittingly named Angela, tended to me. Without warning, the baby's heart rate plummeted and my doctor reappeared at the door at just the right moment. They called a "code blue" and flew my bed down the hall to the OR. I can still remember the look in my husband's eyes as he ran after us. I fought to keep from crying and losing control, again hanging on to the fact that St. Therese had promised this baby would live.

When the doctors operated, they discovered that my womb had ruptured and I was close to death. Suddenly, they ignored the baby to work on my damaged uterus. All the while, I closed my eyes and prayed fervently to God to send His angels to help us. It was a full forty-five minutes before they finally delivered the baby and placed her on oxygen. I can remember my husband announcing with a catch in his voice, "Her name is Grace *Therese*."

They brought Grace with her oxygen over to see me. I felt as though my life were ebbing away. The obstetrician then told us they were having trouble stopping my bleeding. He advised a cesarean hysterectomy, although it was a highly risky procedure. My husband and I looked at each other and knew this meant we would no longer be able to bear souls from God, but there was no choice. Three hours after surgery began, my doctor declared the bleeding had stopped. The relief in the OR was audible.

That night, my nurse, Angela, told us she had never seen a couple with more faith and composure in the face of such intense circumstances. She also had never seen a patient survive such a serious rupture. My OB informed me upon discharge that most women die even if the rupture occurs in the hospital. He told me, "You must have angels around you." My cousin's words suddenly echoed in my head.

Amazingly, my OB told me afterward that they discovered my womb had actually torn apart during the pregnancy and knit itself back together with a protein-like substance. He declared it unheard of in medicine. All I can say is we are profoundly moved and deeply touched by the graces and miracles that have occurred in our lives. We are humbled that God would allow St. Therese to touch us so personally. When I gaze at her picture in my bedroom and look deeply into her eyes, I feel that I know her. Indeed, I do know her, in my heart of hearts. I know that she was present in my hospital room on October 1, 1996, when Christopher John, our rose from heaven, was returned to his heavenly abode. She is true to the promise she made before death, "I will come down!"   — *Deirdre, California*

Pneumonia

It was the winter of 1926, long before the routine use of antibiotics, that my parents asked the Little Flower to make me well. I was a baby, hardly more than a year old, when I developed a case of pneumonia. The doctors held little hope that I would recover.

My uncle in those days had become very interested in a brand new saint, Therese of Lisieux. Many cures were attributed to her intercession. My uncle had recently joined the newly formed Society of the Little Flower, and he took advantage of sending them his prayer intention for my cure. I had been in a coma for two days and, I believe, through the intercession of St. Therese, I awakened, fully recovered, on the third day.

My parents instilled in me from that time on how the Little Flower saved my life. To this day, seventy-eight years later, I still have great faith in St. Therese's curative power.

— *Beatrice, North Carolina*

Prostate Cancer

My husband and I have a great devotion to St. Therese, the Little Flower. Over the years, we have received many favors through her intercession. I'd like to share the most striking one.

Approximately twenty years ago, my husband, John, was diagnosed with prostate cancer. The specialist in Boston that we consulted for a second opinion confirmed what the urologist had told us — John had, at most, two years to live.

Alarmed, we immediately began a novena to St. Therese. About three or four days into the novena, the urologist called to say he would like to do another biopsy before scheduling major surgery. John consented. We continued our fervent prayers.

On the last day of the novena, we were just entering our home after returning from morning Mass when we discovered a single, gorgeous rose in full bloom in our rose garden. We were both surprised, because it was late November, and a typically cold Massachusetts day. There were no other blooms out at this time.

At that very moment, the phone rang and I quickly ran into the house to answer it. It was the urologist. He was calling to tell us that the biopsy was negative. Although he could not explain it, there was no cancer whatsoever. We were both elated.

My husband and I accept this remarkable cure as a miracle from the hands of St. Therese, who promised to shower roses on those seeking her help. To this day, John is in excellent health and has had no symptoms of cancer, thanks to the Little Flower.   —*Lois, Massachusetts*

The Power of Prayer

In 1983, I had been an alcoholic for about eight years. As time went on, this problem was becoming chronic. I was a nurse, and my drinking was affecting my ability to do the job I loved. It was also causing great stress to my family, especially to my father, who was terminally ill and under my care.

I was visiting psychiatrists and going to group therapy, but I felt a great need for spiritual care. I wanted to be at peace and feel God in my life, and to feel like a good person again. During this time, my parish priest was a great source of strength, spirituality, and friendship.

I had always had a great love for Lourdes, a holy shrine I had visited on six separate occasions. There was inside me an overwhelming desire to return, because I felt strongly that I would receive peace in Lourdes. My father gave me the fare to go with some friends who had planned a pilgrimage.

We arrived in Lourdes on July 2, 1983. I was drinking heavily for the first two days. During the trip, an Irish American nun, Sister Elizabeth King, an Incarnate Word Sister, befriended me. She was obviously concerned about my condition. On the evening of July 4, she came with me to the torchlight procession. Again, I was not sober.

After the procession, we went to the Grotto. As we entered it, I noticed a vase of roses at the altar. Impulsively, I took one and handed it to Sister Elizabeth. I did not know she had a devotion to St. Therese of Lisieux or that this gesture would be of great importance. She then told me that she had been praying to St. Therese for me and she always received a rose when her prayers were answered. With that, I felt a tremendous sense of peace and realized my prayers had been answered, too.

I returned to my hotel and poured a bottle of whisky down the sink.

The next morning, I returned to the Grotto with Sister Elizabeth. I thanked Our Lady for bringing me to Lourdes and for bringing Sister Elizabeth, too. I promised Our Lady that I'd never touch alcohol again. I felt so much happiness and joy!

On a subsequent visit
to Lourdes, July 1989

I returned home, fully expecting to have problems with withdrawal and temptation but, miraculously, it was as though the problems had never existed in the first place.

I have never once had the desire to drink in the twenty years since my moment of grace at the Grotto. I thank God and Our Lady every day and often wonder why they gave me such a wonderful gift. I believe my healing was because they love me and they were preparing me for what was to come. The following year I began to suffer terrible depression, due to menopause, that lasted for seventeen years, resulting in early retirement from my work as a nurse.

I know had I still been an alcoholic, I would never have survived those years. In all my bouts with depression, I never once had the desire to drink alcohol. I will be eternally grateful for my miraculous healing.   — *Helen, Scotland*

Campfire Accident

My niece, Jane, had a summer job in a tourist lodge in northern Ontario when she was just twenty years old. After work one Saturday, she stopped to join a number of her friends and fellow workers who were enjoying a campfire. What started as a fun and relaxing evening turned into a terrifying tragedy.

The boss's son, who was tending the fire, decided that the flames were not burning high enough, so he threw on some gasoline. According to the employees, this was something he had done many times before. This time, however, something went terribly wrong. Whether it was due to the air pressure or the wind, no one knows. All anyone can remember is that the gas suddenly caught fire, causing an enormous explosion and igniting into flames everyone sitting nearby.

At the time of the explosion, Jane had been sitting on a picnic table with her back to the fire. In all the commotion, it did not appear to her — or to anyone else — that she was seriously burned. Naturally, those with the most obvious and serious injuries were tended to first. Because of the remoteness of the area, it took a helicopter and a plane ride before Jane and the other victims arrived at the burn unit of a Winnipeg, Manitoba, hospital.

When it was Jane's turn to be examined, the doctors realized that she had burns on 70 percent of her body. Since she had not screamed and cried for help during the crisis, people assumed she was not in serious condition. Through the mercy of God, the first doctor to examine Jane recognized how injured she really was and immediately ordered a tracheotomy. If he had not done so, her neck and throat would have soon swelled to the point of cutting off her breath completely.

The nightmare, however, was only beginning. Jane learned that one of the girls died as a result of this incident, and many others were seriously burned. It was soon determined that Jane would require a long hospital stay in a burn unit where she would face a difficult and very painful road to recovery. In fact, it was almost three months before Jane was allowed to go home. Even then, she had to wear a special pressure suit for over a year to contain the scar tissue on her neck, back and arms.

The physical healing was painful enough, but there was emotional trauma, too. To help with her recovery and uplift her spirits, Jane and a friend came to visit me in November, four months after the accident. When I saw Jane, she was particularly anxious. During the long ordeal, she had received many blood transfusions. She confided to me her intense worry that one of these transfusions could have contained contaminated blood.

I told Jane and her friend that when I am worried about something, I talk to St. Therese. I told them that if you pray for her intercession, you often would receive an answer in the form of a rose. I gave each of them a prayer card with more information.

A couple of weeks later, Jane phoned me from Winnipeg during the day, which was rather unusual. She told me excitedly that something amazing had just happened. While she was at the occupational therapy office, she returned to her chair to discover a rose lying on it. She was stunned. Jane asked everyone in the office if they had seen who had placed the rose on her chair, but no one seemed to know. She was in tears as she told me the story.

Between joyful sobs, Jane let me know that she had been praying to St. Therese every day for two weeks straight. She didn't know anything about novenas; she was just praying fervently that the results of the blood tests would come back clear. The rose on Jane's chair gave her some much-needed consolation that her prayer had been heard. Sure enough, three days later, the results of the blood tests arrived. They were completely clear.

The incident caused Jane to become a believer. She still bears the physical scars of that terrible ordeal and she relived some of her nightmare when she saw the explosion of the Twin Towers in New York on television. But today, Jane is happily married and living in Ireland, where she still prays to St. Therese daily.

Jane believes St. Therese also responded to her prayers for healthy children. It seems that, due to the blood transfusions from the accident, Jane developed an antibody in her blood. Her doctors informed her that this antibody could cause complications in her pregnancies. In the worst-case scenario, this antibody could attack the red blood cells of a developing child, resulting in an intrauterine anemic baby and requiring an intrauterine blood transfusion.

When Jane conceived her first child, the relics of St. Therese were visiting Ireland. Jane went to see Therese's holy remains, and told me later it was as though she could see, touch, and feel the Saint's presence. While there in veneration, she asked St. Therese to help keep her baby protected from her own blood.

The doctors watched Jane's pregnancy carefully. Despite the antibody complication, Jane delivered a healthy baby boy whose only affliction was some jaundice at birth. Two years later, she delivered a perfectly healthy baby girl.

I am proud of my niece, Jane, for how well she has dealt with adversity, and for the wonderful example of faith she is to her family — and to me.   — *Pat, Ontario, Canada*

Joy in the Midst of Suffering

I noticed her thick, shiny red hair, her ready smile, a quiet reverence in her posture and demeanor during Mass, a special poise and peacefulness, and knew this was a woman after my own heart. Terri was a cheerful, upbeat lady who emulated the charm and quiet sanctity of her patron saint, Therese, the Little Flower. I learned in our initial conversation that she was studying to be an Oblate with the Community of St. John. I was interested in the Oblature and had also been considering the life. Terri's friendly ways and deep reverence were part of what attracted me to the community.

I began attending meetings with Terri, but within a few months after I had started she "graduated" and had made her commitment to the community as an Oblate. It was at this time that Terri also asked me to call her Theresa. Theresa decided to take her real name back now that she had become an Oblate, as she felt that through her studies with the Community of St. John, she experienced a deep conversion in all areas of her life. She now felt she was in good company with St. Therese, the Little Flower. I liked the name change, as St. Therese has always been one of my favorite saints. I first learned of her "little way" in my sophomore year of high school. In my English class, her autobiography,

The Story of a Soul, was one of the options for required reading. I loved reading about saints, and once I opened up the
book, I couldn't put it down. What a joyful attitude this
young woman had in the midst of so much pain and suffering! She was unlike anyone I had read about before, and I
admired her.

In December of 2002, something happened that would
change Theresa's life forever. She began experiencing ex-
cruciating pain in her right arm. She sought the counsel of
an orthopedic group, which recommended physical therapy
to strengthen her shoulder, thought to be the cause of the
pain. During the next few months, she exercised and took
a prescribed anti-inflammatory, as the pain continued. In
April, she met with an orthopedic surgeon, who ordered an
MRI, which revealed a mass. A second MRI revealed that
the mass was in her neck and moving in the direction of
her heart. The orthopedic surgeon referred her to a cardiac
surgeon in early May. He ordered more tests: an ultrasound,
a CAT scan, blood work, and a biopsy. Then, on May 12,
2003, Theresa was given the news that she had lymphoma.

Four days later, she saw her oncologist and learned more
of the specifics on her cancer diagnosis and the progno-
sis. Theresa was diagnosed with a non-Hodgkin's lymphoma.
The specific type of lymphoma she was diagnosed with is a
slow-growing one, which often returns after treatment, and
new drug combinations may be required later. A series of
remissions lasting a number of years may occur, and patients
continue their usual activities for very long periods of time.
The minimum number of chemotherapy treatments is six
to eight before any progress in fighting the disease typically
manifests itself.

When I heard of Theresa's illness, I was quite surprised. She had been active, energetic, and looked beautiful. However, I know from personal experience that appearances can be deceiving. I was aware that I needed to do something and that something was to pray.

St. Therese is one of the patron saints of the Community of St. John and also a dear friend to me, like Theresa. I prayed to St. Therese daily for Theresa's healing. St. Therese had come through for me in other difficult situations, and I had faith in her intercession for Theresa.

During this time, Theresa faithfully attended daily Mass at the monastery and prayed to Our Blessed Mother, to St. Therese, and to other favorite saints. Her special intentions were placed on the community prayer line and all of the brothers, sisters, and Oblates were praying for her. Whenever I visited with Theresa, she displayed the same sweetness and cheerfulness she had always expressed. The joy and the inner peace remained intact.

On July 21, Theresa's fourth chemotherapy treatment appointment, she met with her doctor first to compare the results of her initial CAT scan with one that had been done on July 18. He reported that all of the mass was gone, all the lymphs were of normal size, and Theresa was in total remission after just three treatments!

When I asked her how she felt at the time, Theresa replied, "My husband and I just looked at each other. We knew a miracle had happened and so loved Our Lord for seeing us through this. Prayer is so wonderful. I had so many prayers being offered for me, I was so humble and grateful."

I spoke with Theresa the other day. She had just returned from a pleasure trip to Hawaii with her husband. Her conversation was filled with joy, gratitude, and hope for the future.

I asked her about her outlook for the future, and she replied, "I am very positive. I have been through the whole course of treatment. Whatever God puts before me I will handle it with Him. My faith is very strong."

Thank you, Little Flower, for your gracious intercession for Theresa. *—Jean, Illinois*

Theresa Rose

In the fall of 2000, my husband and I learned we were pregnant with our fourth child. My previous pregnancies were normal and healthy. This pregnancy, however, was very different.

During a routine blood test around the eighteenth week of gestation, we discovered to our anguish that there were problems. I immediately began praying to St. Therese. By the twenty-second week of pregnancy, additional tests were confirming alarming complications and we continued praying all the more. I begged our precious Lord for the strength to handle whatever He was sending me, and I implored St. Therese to please intervene for the safety and health of our precious unborn child.

I received several roses during this difficult time as signs that St. Therese was hearing our prayers. It gave me such comfort that, one day, while praying to the Little Flower, I promised her that if the baby were a girl, I would name her Theresa Rose.

Twenty-five weeks into the pregnancy, the doctors told my husband and I that our baby had a better chance of surviving outside of my womb than in it, even though at this point they were predicting only a 5 percent chance of survival. Therefore, on Wednesday, February 21, 2001, Theresa Rose was delivered, weighing a mere fourteen and a half ounces and measuring only ten and a half inches long. As expected, she was born with a host of critical medical conditions.

Theresa Rose stayed in the NICU of Rockford Memorial Hospital under the superior medical care of some outstanding physicians for over four months. She endured five major surgeries to correct a heart problem, a complication of the brain called hydrocephalus, and a vision problem.

During Theresa's hospital stay, her incubator was adorned with tiny statues and novena cards of St. Therese. I always placed one of the statues and a bottle of holy water in the pocket of one of the OR nurses every time Theresa went to surgery.

On July 9, 2001, Theresa Rose came home. We are very proud and happy to say that today, she is a very healthy, very normal two-year-old. The doctors are stunned to say the least. Every day we thank Our Lord and St. Therese for the power of prayer that saved our baby's life. I promised St. Therese I would spread her name and her miraculous intercession for the rest of my life, and I will.

— *Kathryn and Rob, Illinois*

Chapter 6

GUIDANCE

For You are my rock and my fortress;
for Your name's sake You will lead me and guide me.

— Psalm 31:3

And a Child Shall Lead Them

I am a Fourth Degree Knight of Columbus, and a few short years ago I had the honor of standing guard over the reliquary of St. Therese of Lisieux. This began on the night of November 29, 1999, when I had the happy privilege of escorting the Little Flower from the airport to the Carmelite Monastery in Arlington, Texas. How can I begin to describe the feelings that coursed through me for the three days that followed? Excitement, to be sure, happiness, an overall sense of awe, some sadness, and ending with a bit of confusion on my part and a questioning of God's divine plan. But I'm getting ahead of myself.

On that first evening, I stood, transfixed, watching a crew of men uncrate the reliquary. As it came into view a knot instantly formed in my throat, because I knew at that moment I was standing in the presence of a great saint. I looked around to see what effect she was having on everyone else in the hanger. Beyond our group, some curious people were standing in the background in rapt silence and deep reverence. I remember breathing a prayer of thanks to God for allowing me to be there at that moment. The trip from the airport to the monastery was a blur of excitement, and we wondered just how many people would be waiting for our arrival. When we reached our destination the first scene that caught my eye was the nuns standing at the entrance, with their faces all aglow, waiting to greet their sister. I again got misty eyed as I heard the excitement in their voices as they called out, "There she is! There's our Little Flower!" After the greeting prayer was offered, we escorted the relics from the entrance of the monastery to the chapel, and I was amazed at the line of people craning their necks trying to get a better view of this holy visitor.

The next morning I arrived for morning Mass, and afterward stood proudly for honor guard duty. I watched as a long line of people paraded past the reliquary. Some genuflected in prayer seeking intercession, while others just touched the Plexiglas surround in humble veneration. I also longed to touch God's chosen daughter, but I knew that protocol would not allow it. I thought, "Isn't it ironic that I stand before her, less than a foot away, yet she may as well be a mile away." I contented myself by praying to her silently and promising that before she left, I would find some way of touching her.

Later, as my shift ended and I was leaving, a group of children from one of the schools came up to me to talk. The boys, of course, wanted to see my ceremonial sword, while the girls asked me if I planned to be at the convention center for Mass that evening. I assured them that I would not miss it for the world, and I hoped to see them there as well.

As I walked back to my car, a little girl came running up to me and handed me a dime. I looked at her a little puzzled and asked, "What's this for, sweetheart?" She replied, "It's for the Knights of Columbus, sir, because you do good work." I was touched by the generosity of this child. She was obviously moved by the Spirit, and I accepted her gift and thanked her profusely. I handed her my memorial prayer card that I had finally managed to touch to the reliquary at the end of the day, and she ran off to her waiting parents. I multiplied her gift and gave it to my Council, but I kept the original coin for myself. I treasure that coin and keep it in a plastic bag along with the story of its origin.

Knights of Columbus stand guard over the reliquary of St. Therese
Photo credit: Rita K. Tinetti

That night, at the convention center, the excitement began with the arrival of the Carmelite sisters. I watched as they shook hands with the police escort, smiling and waving. The whole evening was beautiful as well, and my family and I enjoyed it very much.

The next day I returned to the Carmelite monastery for more honor guard duty, and I brought with me a medallion bearing the image of St. Therese. I had bought it over a year before, and I wanted to touch it to the reliquary, and did so before the start of my shift. When a Knight stands honor guard, he stands at rigid attention and does not look around, however, it is still possible to see people from the corner of one's eye. On this day, as another stream of people came up to venerate the reliquary, I noticed that many of them were sick or disabled. My heart went out to these people, and I prayed that their prayers would be answered.

Eventually I saw a couple bring up their child in a wheel-
chair. The child was mentally and physically impaired. As
the parents knelt in prayer, I also prayed for this child. She
wore coke-bottle lenses that gave her eyes an almost owlish
look, and I heard her ask innocently as she turned her head
first to one parent, then the other, "What you doing?" "What
you doing?" It was too much for me; I broke down crying at
that moment. I dropped my sword and began fumbling in my
pocket for the medallion. My color corps commander came
running up to see if I was all right. I assured him I was fine
but asked that he let me give this medallion to the child.
I tried to tell the mother it was for the child, but my tears
wouldn't let me. She took the medallion silently without
taking her eyes off the reliquary. I don't know if she realized
what I was doing, and it really doesn't matter. She just took
it and the whole family went their way. I tried to regain
my composure and succeeded, though tears still streamed
down my face. I noticed at this time that my partner, who
was stationed directly across from me, would not look me in
the face. He seemed enthralled by something on the ceiling.
Whatever it was, it must have been some allergen, because
he was sniffling up a storm.

The rest of my tour of duty went pretty much the same
as the first two days. I prayed daily before the reliquary.
I prayed for understanding, because that child's face kept
haunting me. I could not understand why God would allow
this to happen to such a beautiful child. I bid a final farewell
to St. Therese and thanked her for allowing me to stand
for her. I asked for her continued blessings for my family
and me.

A few days later I left for a men's silent retreat in Convent, Louisiana. I was still being haunted by the child's face,

and I found myself questioning God's will more and more. I prayed before the Eucharist and again asked for understanding and forgiveness for my lack of faith. Finally, I went to my confessor, Father Joe, and discussed the matter with him. I remember all I could do was describe the beauty of the child and how she had touched me in a way I'd never been touched before. "Why?" I asked. "Why does God allow such things to be?" Father Joe smiled at me and handed me a Kleenex, because by then I was crying again. He said simply, "You just said it yourself. She, and others like her, were put on this earth for you, so that you could see the beauty of their souls."

A quiet understanding came over me; St. Therese had shown me something very special. She showed me that it was unnecessary for me to be overawed by her as I was. Here was a sweet, beautiful child, whose soul shone through her illness, showing herself to be a living saint. More thoughts came pouring in. The child who had given me the coin, all the people who took part at the reliquary visit, even I myself, we all have the potential of being saints, if we just let God work through us. I thanked Father Joe for his insights and then went to sit outside of the chapel to meditate and thank God for answering my prayer. I thought of St. Therese and her special gift to me, and as I looked up I saw something red just behind the chapel in the garden. Please note it was December, and it was cold outside. What I saw growing on a trestle was a single red rose. I walked up to it with a smile and sniffed it. I thanked St. Therese for her gift but did not pick it. I left it so that someone else who was on retreat would recognize it as his or her gift from St. Therese as well.

— *Sir Knight Lorenzo, Texas*

She Is My Champion

As long as I can remember, I have had a special devotion to St. Therese of Lisieux. I always felt that I
could relate to her. She was young and so devoted to
God. Being young myself, I was comfortable praying for her
intercession.

I grew up in South Jersey and, strangely enough, attended
St. Therese's Roman Catholic Grammar School in Runne-
mede before my dad was transferred to Houston. I always
remember statues of St. Therese holding pink roses.

I was an aspiring figure skater and, over time, it became
necessary for my mom and me to move around the country
so that I could receive the best training possible. It was a difficult situation for our family. There were many times when
I would feel like everything was going wrong — and it was.
Then I would ask St. Therese to help show me the way to
make it better. Sometimes, out of nowhere, I would get pink
roses, and my thoughts went immediately to St. Therese.

In February 1998, I was headed to the Winter Olympics
in Nagano, Japan, to compete. My mom and I were living
outside of Detroit at the time. The day had come for me
to leave for Japan, and we were running late. Mom and I
had to run back to the rink to pick up something that I had
forgotten. In the midst of our rushing, Mom had this feeling
that she needed to check to see if anything had been mailed
to me in care of the rink. This was like a thought out of the
blue, because we had no time to spare to make our plane.

Sure enough, there was a small package that had been
sitting there for a few days. On the way to the airport, we
opened it and discovered it contained two beautiful pink

*Tara Lipinski performing "A Color of Roses," a tribute to St. Therese
Photo credit: Michelle Wojdyla*

roses. They were as fresh as if they had just been cut, but the roses should have been wilted because they were mailed almost ten days before. A priest sent those roses to me, and if ever I needed to get pink roses, it was then.

During the entire Olympic Games, any time I felt stress I would think of St. Therese and those special roses. After I won the gold medal, my first thanks were to this heavenly champion for helping me achieve what I had set out to do.
— *Tara Lipinski, 1998 Olympic Gold Medalist*

Paving the Way

The summer of 1999 marked two full years since my profound journey of faith had begun at the end of my freshman year of college at the University of Nebraska–Lincoln. A very holy and wonderful spiritual director, Monsignor Thorburn, was guiding my conversion of heart.

At least a year earlier, Monsignor had encouraged me to read St. Therese of Lisieux's famous autobiography, *Story of a Soul,* which was the first I had really heard about this Carmelite saint and her "little" book. Agreeably, I picked a copy up at the local Catholic bookstore and found a nice comfortable place for it on one of my bookshelves. For several months I simply glanced at it every now and again, while actually attempting on a couple occasions to dust the top off and begin reading.

I must admit that I was somewhat bewildered as to why Monsignor wanted me to read this particular book as an important aid in my spiritual growth. Honestly, my first impression was that *Story of a Soul* appeared a bit flowery, fluffy, and, well, just plain feminine. I was looking for a more "masculine" spirituality, yet I trusted enough in my spiritual director to know that he had a good reason for recommending this book to me.

My early efforts to read Therese's autobiography all failed without my having made any significant progress. Little did I know just how St. Therese was setting me up within God's exciting and unpredictable providence. In the summer of 1999 I was back home in Sioux Falls, South Dakota, and took up a familiar job driving large dump trucks around for the City Streets Department paving roads throughout the city. Fortunately, as city and construction work often demands, we usually found ourselves sitting around for lengthy periods of time as we waited at the asphalt plant or on the job site. These slow periods provided a prime opportunity for reading, especially since I drove my own truck.

For some reason, the time now seemed right for me to once again take up my year-long struggle of trying to work through *Story of a Soul*. Soon I discovered that the struggle was finally over as I began to effortlessly fly through the pages of Therese's manuscripts. The experience was transforming and quite emotional at times, causing me to tear up more than once underneath my construction hard hat.

Frequently, I would receive visits to my truck from big burly co-workers with sleeveless shirts and foul mouths (while I intently read from a book with the picture of a nun on its front), and naturally they'd ask what I was reading. Usually after the initial awkward look, they were quite willing to listen as I told them about St. Therese and my Catholic faith. One afternoon a fellow truck driver really surprised me when, after breaking into conversation about my passion for the Catholic faith, having used St. Therese and her book as an opener, he very sincerely and seriously shared with me, "Ya know... I think I'll start going back to Mass again."

I was not at all expecting that sort of an immediate response! So, quickly recognizing that St. Therese was at work in a powerful way, I decided to share with him the great value of the Sacrament of Reconciliation as well. He thought that sounded like a pretty good idea too! Ahh... St. Therese is truly amazing, spending her heaven doing good on earth, even in the lives of common construction workers! My spiritual director's wisdom was now clear to me, as was the awesome will of God, who desires to draw souls to Christ through the example and intercession of His beautiful and faithful servant, St. Therese of Lisieux.

—Jeremy, Nebraska

Someone to Look Over My Shoulder

Sometimes life can have some pretty surprising outcomes. If anyone had told me as a child I would one day grow up to be a national Catholic speaker, I would have laughed out loud. I was a most unlikely candidate for such a job but, as we often discover, with God all things are possible. All I know is that God saw fit to keep me in His loving protection by sending someone very special to look over my shoulder.

I was raised by my mother, who was a product of the hippie generation. Her parents had immigrated to America from Germany shortly after World War II. My grandfather was a member of the Nazi party in his youth, while my grandmother was baptized Catholic but raised by a cruel aunt who taught her nothing of her faith. As a result, my mother and I were also baptized into the Catholic Church, but the extent of our religious practice was attending Mass at Christmas and Easter.

As a small child, I was given a statue that I was told was a family heirloom. It came from my maternal great-grandmother. I wasn't told much about the statue and, without a Catholic upbringing, I naturally assumed that it was the image of Mary. After all, the young woman wore a veil and a long dress and held a cross and flowers in her hands.

I never knew quite why, but I always loved that statue. I remember from my earliest years, despite the fact that sexual, physical, and emotional abuse tainted my childhood, it seemed as if this young girl with the pretty smile was watching over me from atop my dresser. Somehow, everything would be okay.

Wherever I lived, I took the statue with me. Even though I did not know or practice my Catholic faith, the sculptured lady seemed to bring me comfort. She was my friend. In college, as a pregnant freshman, she was one of the few friends I had.

I did not discover that my little statue was actually St. Therese of Lisieux until a special woman, a devoted Catholic named Pat, entered my life. She would play a critical role in bringing me back to the faith. When this woman told me she liked my St. Therese statue, I asked, "What St. Therese statue?" She pointed to the figure. I said, "Oh, you mean Mary?" The woman laughed and said lovingly, "No, sweetie, that's not Mary. It's St. Therese of Lisieux." She proceeded to tell me the story of this saint and the miracle of the roses. I was stunned and a little embarrassed. I felt a twinge of strangeness for the first time toward my beloved statue; yet at the same time, I was intrigued to know more about this saint.

At this point in time, I had been searching for deeper meaning to my life through things like crystals, tarot cards, and palm reading. They did not offer, however, what I was seeking emotionally. I had married a Jehovah's Witness, but this faith did not seem to call me, either. My husband's best friend from high school happened to be Pat's son. When the young man introduced his girlfriend to us one day, I adored her from the moment we met. There was a spirituality about the two of them that was very appealing. I was immediately drawn to a beautiful necklace the girl was wearing. She said it was called a Miraculous Medal, and told me the story behind it. I found it fascinating, and was delighted when soon after she presented me with a Miraculous Medal of my own.

As fate had it, my husband and I moved the next month to the town in which Pat and her son lived. One day, while visiting them in their home, they gave me a book about the apparitions of Fatima. I was so moved by the young visionaries' willingness to suffer and the important message of prayer that it prompted me to begin asking questions about the Church. Pat and her son taught me to pray the Rosary, and I began to pray it devoutly. I was not going to church regularly or even really practicing the faith yet, but something was definitely happening, and it continued to escalate from there.

One step at a time, I came to fully embrace my Catholic faith. I discovered the divine mercy of God waiting for all who want to start again. I also discovered the rich treasure of spiritual resources offered by the Church, including sacraments, sacramentals, and the saints. These, unlike crystals and tarot cards, held real, significant, and lasting meaning for me.

Along my spiritual journey, I learned about the Brown Scapular of Our Lady of Mount Carmel and experienced many miracles associated with it. I did not realize at the time that St. Therese was a Carmelite, but I now believe this was one more way the Little Flower was interceding for me. One of the most amazing miracles was bringing my husband into the Church. I had a Brown Scapular blessed and gave it to him as a gift. He wasn't even going to church at the time. After one year of wearing it, he was studying in the R.C.I.A. program! Fittingly, Pat was chosen as his godmother for his baptism.

St. Therese of Lisieux was the first of many saints I have come to love and adore. I enjoy her insight, her piety, and her willingness to suffer and sacrifice. I can particularly relate to her struggle with vanity, as my own attractiveness caused me to stumble many times in my own life. Roses are a favorite of mine; when I smell them on the summer breeze, I think of her still. On more than one occasion, I've prayed a novena and asked for an unusual colored rose only to see a woman holding a dozen roses of that color soon after.

I believe St. Therese has also been very instrumental in giving me the courage to follow God's call to share my life experiences and bring a message of hope to teens. Through the grace of God, I have founded an organization called "Pure Freedom." I travel extensively, presenting my personal testimony to teenagers from coast to coast. In my talks, I share actual experiences and their consequences to emphasize the importance of purity in today's society. I expose destructive forces at work all around teens, including the media, Hollywood, music, and advertising. My goal is to help teens become happier and healthier by learning to see the beauty in relationships with their brothers and sisters in Christ — meaningful and satisfying friendships *without* sex.

The result has been very positive. My live talks and my tapes have apparently helped thousands of teens to take control of their lives physically, mentally, emotionally, and spiritually. In a marvelous way, God has allowed me to bring His love and mercy to His precious children, to let them know they have someone looking over their shoulders, too.

— *Christina, Wisconsin*

St. Therese and My Vocation

When I think of my life, I know I've been blessed. There isn't a doubt in my mind. I grew up in a staunchly Catholic family and providence smiled on me when I was still in the crib. From a very early age I was attracted to the Eucharist in a powerful way, which I believe was because of my parents' direction as I prepared for my First Holy Communion. Among my earliest memories is attending Mass with my parents and the Miraculous Medal novena every Monday night at the cathedral.

My parents were good Catholics, not without their economic and spiritual struggles, but faithful and obviously in love with God. From the moment reason dawned on me, I spoke to God from my heart. I don't know how I knew to do this. I suppose it's best to say that as I was thirsting for God, He was thirsting for me. It was something I recognized — a hunger, a longing that couldn't be filled here on earth. I still feel this. He spoke to my soul intensely, interiorly, and it seems natural that I responded. I came to know Him and to love Him. I spent a lot of time "thinking" as I walked through the countryside, where I spent hours playing by a nearby creek.

My young faith was further strengthened by my second grade teacher, a devout, dedicated Franciscan Sister of Perpetual Adoration from Mishawaka, Indiana. While preparing us for our First Holy Communion, she would patiently and repeatedly with great devotion explain the immense love of God for us in the sacrifice of the Mass and in His perpetual presence in the tabernacle.

I can clearly remember being so moved that it became apparent to me that I should be a priest. The best I can describe it is that I knew — in the second grade, I simply knew. In fact, as a young boy I used to think, "I want to live in the Tabernacle with Him! I never want to be apart from Him." That's the way my childish mind thought. I suppose it seems juvenile now, or syrupy to cynics, but it's what I thought. My mother understood this when I tried to open my heart to another human for the first time. She told me she always hoped I'd hunger for heaven more than anything.

This idea seemed to grow in me: that the vocation to priesthood more than any other would bring me into the closest relationship to the Love I had begun to crave. The unfortunate thing was that as a boy I was extremely mischievous, in and out of minor troubles and constantly inventing new pranks to keep my family "on its toes." I remember crushing an entire box of saltine crackers and putting the crumbs in my parents' pillowcases. Then I'd lie in bed at night and laugh myself to sleep. I hatched a chicken egg once for a science fair and kept the chicken secretly in the house long after I was supposed to give it to a local farmer. My mother came home one day to find the rooster sitting on the kitchen table. My father had only Saturdays in which to try to catch up on sleep. Once I took a ten-pound tomcat and held it above my sleeping father. When his eyes opened, I dropped the cat on my dad. The memories of his screams and the cat howling kept me entertained for days.

During that uncomplicated time, it was one prank after another. I was never in any serious trouble — the closest I came was putting bubble bath in the municipal fountain downtown — but I think my mother knew there was a rocky road ahead. One day, I think maybe in desperation, she told me the story of St. Therese and how she offered God "small things with great love." I was attracted immediately and thought that I could at least do the same, since I knew that I could never manage heroic love with my constant pranks, teasing, and devil-may-care attitude.

Though my pranks and silliness didn't change completely, I found that Therese became a true friend, and over the years this friendship has only deepened. I found it particularly amusing that she had entertained her Carmelite sisters with her own pranks.

Many years passed. I attended six years of Catholic elementary school, followed by public junior and senior high school. I was an exchange student to Europe and finally graduated from a state university. In my sophomore year in college, just months before beginning a year abroad to study in Russia, I definitively decided that I needed to enter the seminary as soon as possible. At the end of the school year, I spoke with the vocation director of the diocese. I was very secretive about my inner thoughts, though I shared them frequently with God, and so when I simply announced one evening at a family gathering that I would enter the seminary in the fall, I remember my father saying, "I give it six months. They won't put up with all the jokes!"

From the beginning of my days in the seminary I went to St. Therese and entrusted my vocation to her. There was a statue not far from the seminary. Every September 30, the anniversary of her death, I decorated the marble flowers in her arms with the petals of roses and marigolds. Her *Story of a Soul* became my spiritual guide, and I, very imperfectly, did my best to follow. My spiritual director at the time poked a little fun at this devotion, calling it sentimental, but I remember thinking that surrender to Love was never sentimental, that in fact it required great strength and was something we could not do alone. I enlisted St. Therese to help me. She must have grown frustrated with me at times! In her *Last Conversations* I loved her complete abandonment and asked God to help me follow this "sure way" of spiritual childhood.

I am certain that the prayers and love of the Little Flower brought me to ordination on May 25, 1985. I have read everything I can get my hands on about her, including an excellent book called *Maurice and Therese*, which did me much good after my mother's death. To this day, Therese and I continue our conversations and her little way of spiritual childhood brings me such joy. One day we will meet in the Homeland, and I will thank her face to face for leading me to know and cleave to Love Himself. I can hardly wait!

— *Father Tim, Indiana*

Picture Perfect

I work in a nursing home in northern New Jersey. In my job, I see life at its best and at its worst. One of the aspects of my job that can be difficult at times is seeing the children of our patients struggle with their parents' illnesses and deaths. I see the way they hurt as they watch their parents gradually ebb away.

Sometimes, the way family members handle these challenges is truly amazing. There is one woman, I'll call her Barbara, whose mother has lived in our nursing home for ten years. The elderly lady can't see or get out of bed. She just smiles at her daughter and eats ice cream. None of this seems to daunt Barbara. She is a retired schoolteacher who has a deep love for Our Lord that is very inspirational to me.

I can't remember how or why Barbara and I started talking about the subject of saints one day, but she happened to mention St. Therese of Lisieux. Even though I didn't know much about the Little Flower, I had a warm feeling inside about her, and our conversation stimulated in me a desire to know more. Barbara started telling me stories about how St. Therese knows when people are praying to her and how she often lets them know she is listening with the sign of a flower. She then gave me a picture of St. Therese along with a prayer card. I was very touched.

I took the picture home and set it, along with the prayer card, on my dresser next to a favorite picture I have of the Shroud of Turin. This picture leans up against a statue of the Infant of Prague that originally belonged to my mother. My mother had a deep devotion to the Infant of Prague and frequently made robes and dresses for its statues before her

St. Therese, the Infant of Prague, and the Shroud of Turin

death. At that point, my aunt was given the statue until she too passed away; then it was handed down to me.

One day as I was cleaning off my dresser and moving the pictures around, I discovered that the back of the prayer card featured pictures of St. Therese that I had not noticed before. One of these pictures was the same exact image that Barbara had given me, which was now sitting on my dresser in front of my Infant statue. Another picture featured St. Therese holding an image of the Holy Shroud — again, the same exact picture that was on my dresser. When I saw this remarkable coincidence, I instantly got a tingling feeling that ran from my head down to my toes. It was awesome. I felt like St. Therese had just spoken to me. But that's not the end of the story.

My new interest in St. Therese caused me to read about her and her relationship with Jesus. One day I was reading a prayer book I had received about St. Therese. To my amazement, it talked about how she loved the Infant of Prague and the Shroud of Turin and how they were all connected, like the set-up I had on my dresser. When I read that story,

I started to cry because I knew that St. Therese had truly contacted me.

It is such an inspiration to pray to these dear departed saints who, from heaven, can really help us today. It gives me an additional sense of security, knowing that we are truly in contact with these holy people of God. Every once in a while, I'll get a rose from someone in answer to my prayers and, when I do, I know it's St. Therese at work. As an added coincidence, my middle name is Rose. Picture that!

— *Elizabeth, New Jersey*

Words of Wisdom

When the AIDS crisis first began, nobody knew what to make of this lethal virus that was killing so many people. In the early to mid-1980s, I did some volunteer work at the hospice at St. Vincent's Hospital in New York City. Originally, the hospice program was geared to cancer patients and their families, but as the dreaded virus progressed and became AIDS, many people who were infected with HIV were admitted to hospice care.

AIDS was becoming rampant, and there was no medication available yet to prolong life. It seemed that once a person was HIV positive, full-blown AIDS would inevitably be diagnosed, soon followed by a horrific, painful, and lonely death.

Perhaps the majority of patients were infected from homosexual behavior, but there were many patients who had acquired AIDS from blood transfusions and other sources. A part of my services was facilitating grief support groups for family and friends who had lost a loved one from AIDS. I remember only too well a mother who wept bitterly over the death of her thirty-five-year-old daughter who had been diagnosed with AIDS after she received a tattoo of a butterfly on her ankle with a contaminated needle.

On October 1, 1985, the feast day of St. Therese, I made a journey out to the Jesuit retreat house on Long Island. There is a small private chapel there, "The Genevieve Chapel," and from the very first time I was in that place, it seemed that St. Therese's presence permeated the chapel. There is a hand-carved wooden statue of Therese there that is different from the likeness we know where she is holding a bouquet of roses. This one was made while she was still "Blessed" Therese, and her hands are folded in prayer.

I prayed in that chapel many times, and for several years it had been my custom to be there on Therese's feast day. This particular day, late in the afternoon, I brought to her my deepest concerns and questions about the horrors of AIDS and the seemingly senseless loss of lives. There was no cure, and no cure in sight. Families were torn asunder; people with AIDS were commonly treated the way lepers were shunned not only during the final days of their lives but after death as well. Often, their bodies were not accepted by funeral directors. In addition, many pastors refused to allow funeral Masses in their churches when someone had died from AIDS, because the disease was aligned with homosexuality, which was contrary to Church teaching, and many Church authorities did not want to court scandal.

By the time the disease was given the name AIDS, my husband and I knew fifteen to twenty people who had either been diagnosed with it, or who had died. On that October 1, I literally begged St. Therese to help me find some way that

I could try to understand it all. My work was focused on these people, and I wanted to help in some way, but I was becoming emotionally depleted and spiritually exhausted. I think I had "bottomed out," as they say.

Before I left the chapel that day, I remember standing in front of the statue of Therese and expressing my feelings in a way that was almost a challenge to her. I let her know my concerns and my frustrations. I candidly shared the anger I felt not only because the disease was spreading like wildfire, but also because the people who had the disease were, in too many cases, being abandoned by their families and relegated to the lowest echelons of society. People who had AIDS were deemed "unclean."

I pleaded with Therese for some enlightenment, a key to try to fathom all of this, something to help me go on with my work. I needed some way of comforting those who were suffering from the disease, and those who were losing their loved ones, often feeling like shamed outcasts themselves. There were so many people who would not dare to admit that a son or daughter, brother or sister, husband or friend had actually died from AIDS. I needed to have some word or sign to help me unravel the kind of desperation I was feeling regarding this horrible disease.

My mind was a kaleidoscope of thoughts: How could any spiritual light lift the darkness that accompanied AIDS? Maybe science would find a "cure" one day, but how could people be at peace now within the horrible reality of such an illness? In a Church whose mission is salvation, how could true healing take place for them?

In the dimness of the late afternoon light in the chapel, I happened to see a copy of a Bible on the chair next to me. I had not noticed it earlier even though I had been in the chapel for several hours. It was a "Jerusalem" translation. I picked it up, held it out to the statue of Therese, glanced at the Tabernacle, and said, "Please...some word...I beg you."

I opened the Bible at random, and when I read the words and the impact became clear to me, my whole body began to shake. The answer to my prayer was given in the words of the Book of Wisdom 5:1–5:

> They will come trembling to the reckoning of their
>   sins,
> and their crimes, confronting them, will accuse them.
> Then, the virtuous man stands up boldly
> to face those who have oppressed him,
> those who thought so little of his sufferings.
> And they, at the sight of him, will shake with coward's
>   fear,
> amazed he should be saved so unexpectedly.
> Stricken with remorse, each will say to the other,
> say with a groan and in distress of spirit:
>
> "This is the man we used to laugh at once,
> a butt for our sarcasm, fools that we were!
> His life we regarded as madness,
> his ending as without honor,
> How has he come to be counted as one of the sons of
>   God?
> How does he come to be assigned a place among the
>   saints?"

Later that evening I received a telephone call from a Maryknoll priest whom I knew. He was a pastoral minister at a hospital, and he was especially saddened because a young man who was dying from AIDS had refused the sacraments. As we talked, I told him about the incident in the chapel and the words I had read, and suggested that the words might give some comfort to the young patient. Two or three days later, the priest called me to say that the Scripture reading had made such an impact on the young man they were able to talk, and that he had received the sacraments before he died.

As days went on, I shared that reading with many people I knew who were involved in working in some capacity with AIDS patients or their loved ones. The comfort and insight of the reading from the Book of Wisdom seemed to make such a difference in so many lives and helped to make many AIDS deaths more peaceful. In the ensuing months, it seemed to me that this verse became the "AIDS" reading, used at bedside, funerals, and memorial services. It was also read at the first Gathering of Franciscans in 1987, where people involved with AIDS ministry on a national level met in Tampa, Florida, for a conference. My husband and I were invited to join them. Ultimately, that first gathering emerged to become the National Catholic AIDS Network.

At a National Catholic AIDS Network conference held at Loyola University in Chicago in 1994, with several hundred people from around the world attending, I was invited to give a workshop on St. Therese of Lisieux and her role (as I saw it) in the AIDS crisis. I shared what I could, including the reading from the Book of Wisdom and the circumstances leading up to my first exposure to these powerful words. I suggested to the groups assembled that perhaps in the writings and life of St. Therese of Lisieux, we can find the key to spiritual healing to cope with this dreaded disease. Perhaps the cure will come one day, but healing on an emotional and spiritual level — as well as some of the insights about the nature of suffering — are all there if only we seek this wisdom. I am thoroughly convinced that Therese will hold the hand of anyone who asks, help him or her to climb the spiritual stairs, and lead each of us home to the Jesus she loves.

— *Anne, New Hampshire*

My Dad's Devotion

My dad was born in 1908, the son of Franco-American parents who had migrated to Maine from Canada. He was the oldest of eight children. His father set up a cobbler shop while his mother set about having and raising children.

My dad would recount with humor how he "graduated" from the fourth grade, by sliding down the rain gutter. At twelve, he went to work in the shoe shop. As was the custom, he gave a large portion of his wages to his parents for "room and board," and the rest he squandered on beer and a shiny new car. It was a bad combination, however, as he demolished the car in his early twenties and never drove again.

My dad was twenty and still working in the shoe shop when he was attracted to a new female worker. This was my mom, a daughter of Canadian immigrants and the oldest of five children. She loved school but had to leave at age sixteen to support her mother and two siblings after her alcoholic father deserted the family. Her mother was in frail health and depended greatly on her for financial support and to help raise the two boys.

When Dad began "wooing" Mom, she made it clear she was not the least bit interested in a drinking, good-time beau. She had seen how alcohol destroyed her own family. Dad had finally met his Waterloo, so much so that he vowed to quit drinking and even joined a sobriety society. Mom accepted this as a serious promise, which it was — in their fifty years of married life, my dad never once took an alcoholic beverage. It was not allowed in our home.

My parents were devout Catholics in their own way. Neither would ever consider missing Sunday Mass and, although prayers were never voiced at home, Rosary beads indicated an active prayer life. They made financial sacrifices to insure me, their only daughter, the benefit of twelve years of Catholic education.

At the time of my parent's marriage, my mom's mother was dying of cancer. They hastened the wedding date, as my dad wanted to assume responsibility of her two brothers. They had little money and furniture was mostly hand-me-downs, but one thing my dad brought to their little apartment was a statue of St. Therese of Lisieux. It was about twenty inches high and the front had a well for a candle. His only explanation was, "This is my statue." Mom never questioned further, respecting his privacy.

I remember that statue so vividly. It always stood on their bedroom bureau and, as the years passed and the paint chipped and her luster grew dull, she still held on to her flowers and her place of honor.

Now there were curious goings-on between St. Therese and my dad, which Mom and I were never privy too. At times she would have a lit candle in the groove at her feet. Other times, we would find her nose stuck to the wall and no candle at all. When dusting, we always returned her to

St. Therese watches over my dad at St. Joseph's cemetery in Biddeford, Maine

the position in which we found her. We assumed that when St. Therese granted my dad his wish, she deserved a candle. At other times, she got put in the corner. This was simply a fact I never questioned, and it wasn't until I was much older that I understood what a tremendous lesson in faith my dad taught me without ever saying a word. Imagine the faith that compelled him to deal with his Little Flower in such a manner. What a lovely open relationship he shared with her.

My dad eventually succumbed to a stroke. I had not been with Mom to the cemetery when she purchased their lot. The day we buried Dad, as I said my teary good-byes, I glanced up to see a tall statue of St. Therese of the Child Jesus two rows away and overlooking his grave site. I do not think this was a coincidence, and I found great comfort in her being near.

The following summer, my husband and I toured the Gaspée Bay in Canada. We stopped at many lovely old churches in quaint villages by the sea, and in a majority of those churches we discovered statues of St. Therese, which brought back fond memories of my dad. I couldn't help but smile every time I lit a candle at her feet.

Over the years, I have acquired my own devotion to the Little Flower and have chosen her to be my prayer partner in intercessory prayer for the souls in purgatory and for the religious serving in the missions. My dad's endearing love affair with this simple servant of God has prompted my spiritual growth. I have often been fortunate to discover roses, or the scent of roses, in answer to prayers, and I know instantly that this special saint has heard and answered. St. Therese has become a part of my life, a special friend, as dear to me as she was to my dad.   —*Muriel, Maine*

The Little Bride

When I first opened the gift from one of my high school students, I was a bit confused. It was a little porcelain thimble, quite delicate and lovely, topped by a tiny bride smiling shyly behind a bouquet of flowers. Although it was charming, I wondered why the student had chosen this particular memento. A great deal of time had passed since I'd considered myself a newlywed. "I guess she just thought it was cute," I surmised, as I thanked her and tucked it away with all the other presents my generous students had given me that Christmas.

When I got home, I put the thimble on the sill of the bay window and more or less forgot about it. It stayed there for years, getting meager attention during an occasional dusting or spring-cleaning. Then, one year, when I got the bug to move things around, I relocated the thimble to my small sitting room where I did a lot of reading and praying. I placed it near a picture of myself with my grandparents, taken decades earlier on my wedding day. It seemed a more appropriate spot than the lonely windowsill in the dining area, and I was quite pleased with the thimble's newfound home and my newfound appreciation of the little ornament. Days later, however, it would garner even greater attention.

It was the quiet morning hours before the bustle of the day really set in, and I was engrossed in prayer. As always, I read the Scripture readings for the day's Mass and meditated on their meaning in my life. Then, as I shuffled through bits and scraps of paper on which I had scrawled meaningful prayers and quotations, I came across a recent addition, something I'd copied from a book at the Carmelite monastery where I volunteer as a portress. I pulled the slip of paper from the ever-expanding stack I sandwiched between the pages of my Bible and reread it slowly.

A simple yet profound thought from the writings of St. Therese of Lisieux, it went like this: "O Little Child! My only Treasure. I abandon myself to your Divine Whims. I want no other joy than that of making you smile. Imprint in me your childish virtues and graces so that on the day of my birth into heaven, the angels and saints may recognize your little bride."

As the beautiful words soaked into my soul, a tiny bell rang in my memory, and I turned my gaze from the page to the long neglected thimble from the past. In an inkling, it took

A prophetic gift from my student
Photo credit: Lanell Marks

on new importance. In that wonderful moment, I suddenly understood that although my student may not have realized her purpose in selecting this gift, the Lord had moved her to do so. After a long season of darkness, a tiny spark of light was finally dawning on its meaning. Like the delicate porcelain figure atop the thimble and like Therese, the Little Flower, I too was the little bride, the spouse of Christ. It didn't matter that I was past middle age, that I was past my first encounter with Him, and past the newness of the nuptial blessing. I was still His little bride, never to be stowed away and forgotten in some obscure, dusty corner, but always bright and visible and highly prized. Maybe I had lost sight of that, but He hadn't. Thanks to the thimble and the prayer of the Little Flower, I realized it afresh and yearned more fervently than ever to renew my wedding vows, to satisfy the whims of the divine Groom, and to watch Him smile.

"Thank you, Jesus," I prayed, "for helping me to discover a treasured truth, locked away for so many years in a tiny thimble." — *Bonnie, Louisiana*

Being Led to Lecture

I am a high school English teacher who retired early on medical disability. One weekend I made a retreat at the Trappist monastery of Our Lady of the Genesee in Piffard, New York, and read for the first time *A Story of a Soul*. During the course of the conferences I attended during this retreat, I was amazed at the ease and facility with which I was able to share thoughts and feelings, to be open and honest, without pretense or facade.

After the retreat, I began lecturing on the life and spirituality of the Saint and doing extensive research on the many books and articles that have been published on her. My lectures met with much success and my research progressed with unflagging interest. The most amazing thing about all of this is that I had never planned it — it had to be God's will for me. This is the fifth year of my continual research on St. Therese.

To further confirm this providential phenomenon, I have experienced a most reassuring sign. One of my prayer books is entitled *Through the Year with St. Therese of Lisieux: Living the Little Way*, by Constant Tonnelier. The cover of this book bears the face of St. Therese of Lisieux. This face actually smiled at me on three different occasions. Surely, it cannot be coincidental.

I have also discovered that many spiritual truths, which my studies in theology and philosophy made very complex, became crystal clear as I perused the writings of this Carmelite nun who lacked a higher education and was not formally trained in theology and philosophy. Even my prayer life and meditations on the Gospel flourished and graces of prayer flooded my soul with interior illuminations and thoughts.

I am praying constantly to the Little Flower that God will grant me a vocation to the priesthood if this is His holy will for me. In this prayer, I echo the words of St. Therese of Lisieux, "My God, I choose all that Thou willest."

— *Ronald, New Jersey*

A Heavenly Friend

In 1997, two seemingly unrelated events occurred. Pope John Paul II named St. Therese of the Child Jesus and the Holy Face a Doctor of the Church, and I turned fifty, a time of looking back and inevitably forward.

The juxtaposition of these two events renewed my interest in this saint whose name I had chosen as my Confirmation name and patron saint in the late 1950s. What did she have to say to me after all these years?

It was not that I had lost interest in her altogether. I had a sentimental interest in her from my religiously intense childhood. Also, my mother had chosen Therese as her Confirmation name and was so pleased when I followed in her footsteps. Likewise, my future mother-in-law had chosen her and so did some of my dearest friends. Sharing the same name with these women felt like a special bond between us, but it went no further. In later life, none of these women, to my knowledge, had a well-developed devotion to St. Therese, and despite some tepid attempts at connecting, neither did I.

A sweet saint, a pure spirit, of this I was sure. But a Doctor of the Church? I never would have expected that. She was so young when she died and so isolated from the sufferings that accompany life in the real world. I wanted to find out why she was accorded this honor given to only thirty-three saints in the entire history of the Church.

There was plenty of material to explore, many books containing her personal story, letters, and poetry, her contemporaries' records of conversations, historical details and deliberations on them. One of the most meaningful books to me was the correspondence between St. Therese and the young seminarian Maurice Belliere. I was moved by her warmth and enthusiasm on his behalf, despite the fact that she was very near death herself. But most important, in her words I could see that part of her had already gone to God and understood the intercessory role she would play in the future.

Maurice wrote to Therese, saying that while she might be able to bear with him on earth, she might not after death: "But in heaven, where you will share in the Divinity, you will take on its prerogatives of justice and holiness, and everything that is sullied will become an object of horror for you."

She responds so beautifully: "You think that, once I share in the justice and holiness of God, I won't be able to excuse your faults as I did when I was on earth? Are you then forgetting that I shall also share in the infinite mercy of the Lord? I believe that the Blessed in heaven have great compassion for our miseries. They remember that when they were weak and mortal like us, they committed the same faults themselves and went through the same struggles, and their fraternal tenderness becomes still greater than it ever was on earth. It's on account of this that they never stop watching over us and praying for us."

In her words, I saw the theological virtue of hope embodied. St. Therese understood heaven even down to some details, the special efficacy God would grant her on behalf of those for whom she would pray. She wrote, "The saints encourage me from above, they say to me: 'So long as thou art in fetters thou canst not fulfill thy mission; but later, after thy death — then will be the time of thy conquests.'"

St. Therese is talking about a love that transcends death yet remains personal, a Communion of Saints that is ours if we believe. What a gift! What comfort! This is not sentimental piety; the words of a child isolated from real life. Rather, these are the words of a mature spirituality witnessing to a revered doctrine of the Church and offering us an opportunity to enter her life with Christ.

I have found many other sound reasons why St. Therese was named a Doctor of the Church, but this one is special to me. It has restored some of the innocent faith of my childhood. I now think I have a friend in heaven. Her name is Therese.   — Maryanne, New York

"*I will return! I will come down!*
I want to spend my heaven doing good on earth."

SUGGESTED READING

Fortunately for us, there is a vast array of books published about St. Therese of the Child Jesus and the Holy Face. The following titles are recommended to enhance your knowledge of this special saint. It is by no means a comprehensive or definitive listing.

Ahern, Patrick. *Maurice and Therese: The Story of a Love.* New York: Doubleday, 1998.

De Meester, Conrad. *St. Therese of Lisieux: Her Life, Times and Teaching.* Washington, D.C.: ICS Publications, 1997.

———. *With Empty Hands: The Message of St. Therese of Lisieux.* New York: Continuum, 2000.

d'Elbee, Jean C. J. *I Believe in Love: A Personal Retreat Based on the Teaching of St. Therese of Lisieux.* Manchester, N.H.: Sophia Institute Press, 2001.

Gaucher, Guy. *The Passion of Therese of Lisieux.* New York: Crossroad/ Herder & Herder, 1998.

———. *The Story of a Life: St. Therese of Lisieux.* San Francisco: HarperSanFrancisco, 1993.

Guitton, Jean. *The Spiritual Genius of St. Therese of Lisieux.* Westminster, Md.: Newman Press; London: G. Chapman, 1958.

Keating, Thomas. *St. Therese of Lisieux: A Transformation in Christ.* New York: Lantern Books, 2001.

Martin, Celine (Sr. Genevieve of the Holy Face). *My Sister St. Therese.* Rockford, Ill.: Tan Books & Publishers, 1997.

O'Mahony, Christopher, ed. *St. Therese of Lisieux by Those Who Knew Her (Testimonies from the Process of Beatification).* San Francisco: Ignatius Press, 1989.

Therese of Lisieux, St. *Letters of St. Therese.* 2 vols. Translated by John
    Clarke. Washington, D.C.: ICS Publications, 1988.
————. *Poems of St. Therese of Lisieux.* Translated by Alan Bancroft.
    New York: HarperCollins, 1997.
————. *The Poetry of St. Therese of Lisieux.* Translated by Donald
    Kinney. Critical Edition of the Complete Works of St. Therese
    of Lisieux, Centenary Edition 1873–1973. Washington, D.C.: ICS
    Publications, 1996.
————. *St. Therese of Lisieux: Essential Writings.* Edited by Mary
    Frohlich. Maryknoll, N.Y.: Orbis Books, 2003.
————. *St. Therese of Lisieux: Her Last Conversations.* Translated by
    John Clarke. Washington, D.C.: ICS Publications, 1977.
————. *Story of a Soul: The Autobiography of St. Therese of Lisieux.* 3rd
    ed. Translated by John Clarke. Washington, D.C.: ICS Publications,
    1999.
————. *Thoughts of St. Therese: The Little Flower of Jesus, Carmelite of
    the Monastery of Lisieux, 1873–1897.* Rockford, Ill.: Tan Books &
    Publishers, 1992.
Tonnelier, Constant. *Through the Year with St. Therese of Lisieux: Living
    the Little Way.* St. Louis, Mo.: Liguori Publications, 1998.

Do you have a St. Therese story
you would like to share?

Please send it to Elizabeth Ficocelli at

ashowerofroses@sbcglobal.net

Of Related Interest

Rudolf Stertenbrink
THE WISDOM OF THE LITTLE FLOWER
Thérèse of Lisieux — Bearer of Modern Spirituality

Beloved Saint Enters the Mainstream!

Millions of people around the world, including the pope, are devoted aficionados of a modest young nun who died early last century. What is the secret of Thérèse of Lisieux, who is one of only three women to be awarded the exclusive title of "Doctor of the Church"?
St. Thérèse of Lisieux believed that what matters most in life is not high theology, but hope against all adversity. In this engrossing book, Stertenbrink unearths the more thoughtful side of this simple nun. In doing so, he quotes from Dostoyevsky, Kierkegaard, Cardinal Newman, and Edith Stein, among others. The result is a direct encounter with Thérèse. The book comprises short essays that can be read one at a time — before bed or on the train — or straight through for a compelling narrative.

978-0-8245-1983-4

Guy Gaucher
THE PASSION OF THERESE OF LISIEUX

"Bishop Gaucher's haunting account of Thérèse's final eighteen months ... reveals her at the summit of her journey, when she became a unique masterpiece of God's amazing grace, and the saint for the next millennium." — *Bishop Patrick V. Ahern, D.D.*

Few saints enjoy the popular devotion of Thérèse of Lisieux. It is well known that this twenty-four-year-old Carmelite died of tuberculosis while unpetalling roses, but what was her life really like during the critical last months? This volume is the definitive history compiled from Thérèse's letters and manuscripts written during this period.

978-0-8245-0987-3

crossroad

Of Related Interest

Robert Ellsberg
ALL SAINTS
Daily Reflections on Saints, Prophets, and Witnesses for Our Time

Winner of the 1998 Christopher Award

From Thérèse of Lisieux to Mother Teresa, from Moses to Gandhi, this inspiring treasury combines traditional saints with other spiritual giants whose lives speak to the meaning of holiness for our time.

"A wonderfully broad, knowing, and narratively compelling look at human goodness as it has been tested by life. This book will give us the very best kind of moral and spiritual education."   — *Robert Coles*

ISBN 978-0-8245-1679-6

Support your local bookstore or order directly
From the publisher at www.CrossroadPublishing.com

To request a catalog or inquire about
Quantity orders, please e-mail
sales@CrossroadPublishing.com

crossroad